MW01240992

DON'T
TELL ME
TO CALM DOWN

FACE YOUR POWER
AND
FIND YOUR PEACE

ERIN DONLEY

ERIN DONLEY COMMUNICATIONS
PORTLAND, OREGON

This book is dedicated to my best friend, Suzi.
Thanks for never being offended.

CONTENTS

ACKNOWLEDGMENTS

Writing a book requires a ridiculous amount of support. These people crossed the finish line with me, and I'll forever be grateful.

Christy Weber, thanks for your quality editing and superior eye for detail. You calm me down when I need it most.

Omkari Williams, you are the epitome of fierce compassion, and your feedback made all the difference in my confidence.

Ingrid Kincaid, thanks for teaching me how to tell the truth when it's hard and when people don't want to hear it. Our friendship means more than I can express.

Patricia Evans, thanks for your dedication to verbal abuse education. Your strength in the face of pain helps all of us do the same.

Thanks to New Renaissance Bookshop for giving me a start as a writer and the freedom to find my voice over the years.

Tim Brown, thanks for killing me with laughter and walking the same speed as me. You fueled me through this project.

Thanks to everyone who offered wisdom and encouragement:

Suzi Caffreys, Jackie Donley, Shawn Donley, Naomi Dunford, Keri Caffreys, Üma Kleppinger, Dr. Carin' Bocskay, Caelan Huntress, Riley Hayes, Eric Seminara, Della Rae, Allison Clarke, Rob Siebens, Clarissa Smith, Rachel Beohm, Cherie Collins, Erin Keys, Renee Graziano, Karen O'Neill, Beth & Mike Spinning, Doug Zanger, Lesley Feingold, Derek Lewis, David Prouty, Monica Marteau, Dr. Joyce Follingstad and everyone at therapy group, and always, thanks to my family.

Special thanks to Neil Young for speaking my language when I couldn't find the words.

"Not everything that is faced can be changed, but nothing can be changed until it is faced."

— James Baldwin

PROLOGUE

When I first met Dee, she'd been trans-
ferred from her home in Las Vegas to
an adult care facility in Portland, Oregon, where she
would wait out her final months of life. Although she
was diagnosed with multiple sclerosis years earlier,
Dee was dying from nonalcoholic cirrhosis of the
liver at age 64.

Family support for Dee was challenged. Her
daughter and grandchildren lived across the country. Her son was nearby but was exhausted from
trying to make her calm and comfortable—a
seemingly impossible task. He needed an ally,
someone to take charge when he couldn't. He
also needed a companion for Dee, someone to

hang out with his dying mom who was isolated and withdrawn.

Before walking into her room, I learned that Dee's husband had recently passed away. Ironically, he was a heavy drinker, yet it was Dee's liver that took the beating with cirrhosis. Their marriage lasted over 40 years. They were committed, but contentious.

At the time of meeting Dee, I was at a low point in my life, too. Big changes had to be made in my relationship, home, and career, but I was afraid to face them. In desperation, I reached out to a teacher who taught a class about death in America. While a student in her six-month course, I recalled she ran a consulting business for families with dying loved ones. Dee had just become her new client.

I was asked to become Dee's companion for 6–8 hours per week at an hourly fee. It wasn't a lucrative proposition, but it was a short-term escape from my problems and a chance to explore what it's like to be around the dying, which has always been of interest to me. Most days, I sat next to Dee with my feet propped on the rails of her bed, and we'd chat away like old friends. I was also her travel buddy for doctor's appointments and hospital visits.

"How ya doin' today, Dee?" asked every nurse, doctor, and therapist. On my first day, I noticed that regardless of her answer, they all would attempt to be uplifting: "Oh, sorry to hear that. Just try to relax." Any pain she felt, "Just try to relax and calm down." Any concerns she had, "Just relax. Everything's going to be fine."

I realized right away how much the suggestion to "relax" pissed her off. Unfiltered disgust would cross over her face when she heard it. It didn't take a genius to realize, if I was going to earn her trust and be allowed to stick around, it would never, ever be appropriate for me to tell her to relax. Yet, I could see why these people were suggesting it.

Dee's irritation was palpable. Her feet hadn't hit the floor in almost a year. She was bedbound—unable to stand, walk, pull herself up, or use the bathroom on her own. Dee was a large woman, and for transfers into her wheelchair, we had to use a hydraulic Hoyer lift, which was a tremendous ordeal. She wouldn't leave the bed for weeks at a time. That dreaded lift was the bane of her existence.

Sadly, a quarter-sized bedsore had formed at the tip of her tailbone. It oozed with infection that would not (and could not) heal. When she was lifted from bed, her body weight would rest on the sore, and she would scream in agony. Without telling her to "just relax," I could only stand there and pray. Those moments sparked gratitude for the healthy functions of my body.

At one point, she told me something strange: "When they changed the dressing on my bedsore, there's no other way to describe it . . . it smelled like death." Wow, I wondered if that meant the end was near. We never knew exactly when she was going to go—doctors estimated six months. She talked to her caretaker about the ominous odor. It was vehemently denied: "Oh, that's absurd, Dee! That's not what it was. You're fine."

When that woman left the room, Dee said, "See what I have to deal with? Since I've become sick, no one believes anything I say." In that moment, I vowed to believe her every word, no matter how gory, scary, or negative it might be. It was the end of her life, and she had quite a lot to say. Because I wasn't a close friend or relative, nothing she could say would offend me. Dee understood that and felt safe to express whatever she wanted.

We had six glorious months together of bitching up a storm. When I'd walk through the door, Dee would grin and then launch into a story of oppression from her past. She had a lifetime of gripes about her degenerate brother, incompetent doctors, commanding husband, rude bosses, nosy neighbors, and dominating mother-in-law whom she described as a "ball-buster and a half!"

Dee was silenced, shunned, and shamed all her life. These instances were still alive in her, and she wasn't about to die until she recalled each one and named what was wrong about the encounter.

As the youngest in the family and the only girl, Dee resented how everyone claimed to know what was best for her. They instructed her on how to act and expected her to be pleasantly compliant. If she questioned their judgment, she'd be ridiculed. If she showed her strength as a woman, they'd tell her to tone it down.

Dee fought against these forces with undeniable victories. Those were her most repeated tales. The telling of her stories became a battle cry for me to wake up and see where I, too, had lost my sense of power. When had I allowed others to define who and what I should be? When was I told to "just relax" when exerting my perspectives?

Since Dee was dying (and there was nothing we could do about it), we didn't try to fix, save, or correct each other. We simply let things suck when they sucked. We'd even go into detail about why something sucked as bad as it did. For us, this was honest and therapeutic—creative even. It was a release.

Dee and I rode out her time with as many laughs as possible. I brought her flowers and painted her fingernails. We munched on caramel corn, shared recipes, gossiped about celebrities, and joked about the day we'd have guacamole, chips, and margaritas together. Salt on the rim!

At an urgent care trip where they had to weigh Dee, she realized she had lost over 100 pounds. Like a contestant on a makeover show, Dee pumped her fists with pride. Her digestion had been a disaster and food was no longer her friend, but her declining weight still thrilled her. She joked, "This year, I'm definitely going to my class reunion!"

When I was with Dee, it felt so liberating to turn off my phone, leave my personal needs aside, and tune into another person's world. When I'd tell people about how much fun we had together, many would shrivel and ask me to stop mid-sentence.

Prologue

Some even thought it was twisted that I enjoyed being around a dying person. The negativity that surrounds death, which is an inevitable and natural part of life, was too much for them. They'd look at me with pity, like I didn't have enough respect for myself to choose a more uplifting environment. Clearly, they couldn't see or recognize my sincere contentment.

Towards the end, Dee started having frequent hallucinations. With cirrhosis, the liver becomes like scar tissue and is unable to filter toxins. That causes a gaseous buildup, an ammonia-like substance that travels to the brain and causes delusions. Some of these visuals were wildly entertaining. She saw gorillas swinging from trees, heard mariachi bands playing in the night, and talked about the raging parties next door where a quiet, elderly couple lived. "Yep, the cops had to break up the scene again. Those people are out of control!"

The detail in her stories was hysterical; however, some were downright terrifying as if straight from a horror movie—cigarette butts burning in her bed, evil-looking children kneeling down in the corner staring at her. Those stories she would whisper out of fear.

Dee openly discussed what she saw, but everyone insisted the visuals weren't real: "It's not really happening, Dee. It's just your mind playing tricks on you. We'll adjust your meds." My boss told me to try something else—listen, believe her, and empathize. That felt easier, kinder, and way more authentic. Had I questioned her sanity or tried to make her see the positive, she would have felt even more agitated.

In the last few weeks with Dee, *my* life started to turn around. I dropped a few pounds, got into an exercise groove, and moved away from my home and relationship. Career-wise, I landed my first ghostwriting book contract with a high-profile leader in finance. This allowed me to quit juggling part-time jobs and start a whole new chapter—one that I badly needed.

I didn't share much with Dee, but she knew I was seeking my first ghostwriting client. When I told her I closed my first deal, she became quiet. "Well, I'm happy for you," she said, "but you need to write a book for people like me . . . people who don't take anyone's bullshit and refuse to be fake."

Dee suggested we call the book, "Don't Tell Me to Relax!" Knowing how demeaning those words were to her, I promised to make it happen one day.

My mother proposed the slight change in wording, "Don't Tell Me to Calm Down." She said, "No one has ever calmed down from being told to calm down. In fact, I get even angrier." Yep, the apple doesn't fall far from the tree. It delights me to write a book that Dee inspired and my mother has named.

Dee's story is largely about the gift of being present for someone's pain. When I met her, I needed to make some tough, life-altering decisions. Seeing her suffer and hearing her stories of oppression helped me do it. I didn't need someone to cheer me on, and I didn't need to surround myself with optimistic people; I needed to see how unendurable my life would remain if I didn't take action.

On the day Dee died, I rested her hand on my lap. If she felt warm skin, I thought, maybe she'd know there was a person there for her final breaths. At this point, she was unable to talk or make eye contact. Her son arrived at the home, and I stepped outside to finish writing her obituary. When the final period was typed, I looked up from my laptop. Her caretaker announced Dee was gone. That synchronicity *still* gives me chills!

As I re-entered her room, Dee's son stood up and gave me a hug—possibly the most potent embrace

I've ever had. An unexplainable rush, more like a jolt, blasted through my body. It was as though Dee had her celestial arms around us, offering a grandiose goodbye. She was finally free, and although I would miss her, I was relieved she had escaped her painful, broken-down body.

I believe she died better (if there's such a thing) for having been given the chance to openly complain about what hurt, angered, and saddened her. With guidance from my boss, we were able to validate Dee's experiences, instead of crushing them with forced optimism or demands to "relax."

She needed to express her regrets out loud and make sure someone *knew* how much she endured, how much she survived. It was an honor to be on the receiving end of those words.

In the end, we were both set free.

INTRODUCTION

World-renowned genius Albert Einstein said, "Stay away from negative people. They have a problem for every solution." That quote was liked by millions on social media. Similarly, there was another post that became popular, "Three types of people to stay away from: The uninspired, unexcited, and ungrateful."

If you gain only one thing from this book, let it be this: These statements have a seemingly innocent and uplifting tone, but their impact is often demoralizing. For each person who has been helped by this kind of inspiration, far more have been hurt by it.

How do I know? Well for starters, Dee was all of these things—negative, uninspired, unexcited, and ungrateful—yet, being in her presence was tremendously positive. Had I stayed away from "people like her," I might have never written this book or made the changes I needed at that time.

I also had the fortune of being a manager at a gigantic, personal growth bookstore in Portland. This isn't a hole-in-the-wall bookshop, it's the self-help mecca of the Pacific Northwest. Attached to the store is an event center for transformational workshops. For nearly a decade, I was surrounded by the who's who of self-development.

Book readers were my primary focus. I wanted to understand the psyche of these shoppers and anticipate their obvious and unspoken needs. What I learned provided a revolutionary discovery that eventually led me to become a ghostwriter for authors wanting to write their own leadership, activism, or self-help books.

Each day at the store, customers would pull me aside. These were people from various genders and backgrounds who'd make the exact same comments. They would start out by saying, "I don't know what's wrong with me . . . I'm embarrassed to tell you . . . It's frustrating to share this, but . . . "

Whatever they were about to say carried shame and defeat.

They'd elaborate, "I've tried to be peaceful and loving, but I can't stay there for long. I want to 'let it go,' but my brain refuses to forget. I've tried the Law of Attraction and gratitude journals, but I can't seem to make them work. Is there anything for people like me?"

I'd hear the most jaw-dropping stories about illnesses, setbacks, betrayals, and losses—discrimination due to gender, age, religion, sexuality, race, income, and body weight. You would think I'd be drained at the end of the day, but instead I'd feel restored. Hearing what was *honestly* occurring in people's lives was like drinking the purest water on the planet. After years in corporate sales, I was thirsty for real talk and transparency.

When they'd finish talking, I could hardly wait to tell them how *normal* they were and how everyone was pooped over the pressure to be perky. This relentless aim to be positive had created a collective sense of exhaustion, especially in the workplace. People were terrified of being labeled "negative."

I'd tell them, "Not everyone likes my choice in books, but if you're open to the idea of having stronger boundaries, if you want your comfort zone to be challenged, or if you'd like to examine your *range* of emotions, I have some suggestions."

The books I chose for them were designed for deep resolution—topics such as trauma, intimacy, sexuality, death and dying, addiction, shadow work, psychology, and conflict resolution. Weeks later, they'd come back to thank me.

My favorite book to recommend was *Controlling People: How to Recognize, Understand, and Deal with People Who Try to Control You* by Patricia Evans. Instead of encouraging folks to simply see the best in others, it gave me such pleasure to hand them a book that might explain the root cause of their confusion and pain.

Soon after this job began, I started writing an email newsletter to the store's customer database. Each week, I'd choose a book, interview the author, and position this product in the most irresistible way possible.

Each time we'd hit 'send,' book sales and customer interaction would kick into gear. People would reply with their most pressing (and personal) issues. At times, it was overwhelming. They'd visit the store or track me down on the streets so I could prescribe their next self-help book. It was an exhilarating phase of my career. I loved supporting authors who dared to be different. I loved being part of a tight-knit team. I loved people's honesty.

Every vulnerable story boosted my crusade against "oppressive positivity," which is the belief that positive people and optimistic attitudes are required for happiness, success, and healing to occur, and that we should revere those who achieve this eternal state of cheerfulness and strive to do the same.

That is a lie that's constantly being fed to us. It's a myth supported by groupthink. You no longer need to digest falsity because it sets an unreasonable standard for society. All feelings are valid and necessary. The key is to skillfully manage the difficult ones.

"Avoid negative people. They have a problem for every solution."

Do you see how potentially hurtful that statement can be? It suggests *some* people deserve to be shunned if they're in pain. It says you need others to act a certain way, even if they have to pretend. It says your range of acceptable emotion is limited.

In this book, we'll start by looking at what situations yank your irritation chain. After confronting how you feel about others, you'll be ready to examine your relationship to yourself. The strategies you'll learn won't allow you to wallow in victimhood or anger. They'll show you how to find clarity, move on, and compartmentalize that which is still unresolved in your life.

Let's get started.

CHAPTER 1

HOW TO BE PRESENT FOR ANOTHER PERSON'S PAIN

What happens when you're around someone who is negative? Do they make you feel uncomfortable? Do you wish they'd go away? Do you try to quiet them down? Do you feel tired after spending time with them? Do you avoid those in physical, emotional, or mental distress?

Here are a few tactics to open your empathy and build your resilience around those who may appear to be in agony. If you don't want to be told to 'calm down,' you have to learn how to extend the same courtesy.

Get educated about those who are different.

In order to be safe for a person in pain, you must study the plight of those who are different from you. Read books, watch movies, go to plays, or listen to podcasts from people of all genders, ages, races, locations, and economic classes. Expose yourself to various points of view. Discover what are considered common fears and universal pain points.

Recently, I listened to a podcast about depression with Ezra Klein. His guest Johann Hari discussed one key factor causing stress-related heart attacks and depression at work—it's the feeling of being controlled in your job. We need our lives to be meaningful, and when we lack control, it disrupts our ability to find that meaning.[1]

I mention this study because it allowed me to contemplate what may be happening when someone complains about their crappy boss or unfair work policies. Instead of hearing them as whiners, I listen for how it's taken a toll on them to constantly relinquish control. This insight can help you accept people's struggles and see what they may be facing, both in life and in work.

It's also important to learn the normalized behaviors and often subtle words and phrases that allow sexism, racism, misogyny, xenophobia, homophobia, or antisemitism to keep existing. Discrimination becomes the norm when it isn't carefully examined. Inform yourself, if anything, to be sure your unconscious biases cease to cause harm.

- Find a class in diversity, equity, and inclusion.
- Buy books written by people of color.
- Study feminism and the history of black women in America.
- Learn how oppression works, and how it stays alive.
- Request training in these topics at work.

Find me online if you want to delve into these subjects more. I'm connected to some incredible leaders who are fighting hard against hatred in all forms.

Drop the labels.

Instead of categorizing people as positive or negative, which are polarizing labels, try to see a person for everything they are.

For example, you notice a friend is funny and bright, but they're also long-winded and self-absorbed. Instead of seeing these as negative traits that must be avoided, process this as simply "information." At times, this person might seem annoying, but at other times, it might feel relaxing to sit back, listen, and say nothing.

If you need to chat about a problem in your life, realize this person's inability to reciprocate. Accept it. Don't set yourself up for disappointment and don't set them up to fail. Choose your time with them wisely based on your moods. See the variety of shades this person can offer, instead of pigeon-holing them into good/bad, right/wrong.

Set boundaries to protect yourself.

Depending on your relationship with a person, you might want to set limitations on how much you can give. If a coworker wants to vent, you can say, "I have five minutes, and they're all yours." Politely excuse yourself when the time's up. You can even say, "I'm going to set a timer to keep myself on track." When it dings, make the first move to wrap up the conversation.

If the person wants to complain about someone, and you don't want to participate, be sympathetic to the person having the problem. Your friend might be mad that a loud neighbor woke their newborn child. Focus on how it affected them. "Oh, that sounds brutal. You must be bone-tired today!" You don't have to criticize the accused perpetrator along with them. That's when it can turn negative for you.

After a client leaves, therapists will often burn candles, open windows, drink water, spray rose water, or go for quick walk. When you leave someone who's in crisis or despair, take a moment to break up that energy in your body and in the room. The sights and sounds of a person who's in pain can stick with you, so take extra care of yourself.

Don't make it about you.

When we hear people's pain, we often respond with the phrase, "I know exactly how you feel! That happened to me, too." We crave connection, and it helps to know we're not alone. But for the purposes of being safe for someone who's in pain, place your attention on the other person. When we constantly chime in with our views, it's called centering. In your time with this person, relinquish the desire to focus on yourself.

Clarify how you can help.

When you hear people vent about their partner or grumble about politics, instead of telling them to get over it or look for the positives, get clear about how you could be most helpful. These questions can keep them trusting you as a confidant.

Would you like me to just listen?

Are you open to hearing my thoughts on this?

Would you like to brainstorm this together?

What are you afraid will happen?

What do you need most right now?

Let people express their pain.

Carl Jung said, "Loneliness doesn't come from having no one around you, but from being unable to communicate the things that are important to you." We need people to hear what's dear to us—the thoughts we hold close.

Encourage people to tell you more and to describe how they feel. Tell them it's great to hear them release frustration or get this off their chest and that you're sorry for the pain this is causing them.

Be cautious when encouraging positive thought. It has its place, but it also has the power to minimize. As tension builds in response to someone's heartbreak, betrayal, or regret, can you simply be present for it?

At times, we minimize people's pain by making a joke of what happened or trying to laugh off the discomfort. This may be just what's needed to soften the hurt and distract their thoughts, but make sure you have already established trust with that person. Humor is appropriate if there's trust. Otherwise, it can be awkward and distasteful.

Don't try to fix or save them.

There's a classic book from the 80s called *Women Who Love Too Much*. It sat on the shelf in my childhood home, and I wondered how someone could possibly love too much. I learned as an adult, it's called codependency—the belief that our love can have the power to change people. There's a 12-step program for codependency, and I've found some of the most confident people I know have worked hard at keeping their codependency in check.

After a friend's surgery, her family swooped in with healthy smoothie recipes, cleansing diets, and a list of naturopathic doctors. While my friend appreciated the resources at first, it became a problem when she didn't take action on what was recommended. She was blamed for not doing enough to fix herself. She was criticized for not taking these actions that were labeled "positive" by her relatives. When I stopped by to visit, she said, "All I want is for you to sit here with me and say nothing."

As loving humans, we want to provide solutions for each other, but no one likes receiving unsolicited feedback. Get in the practice of asking, "Would you like my take on that?" or "Are you open to a few ideas?" Allow people to say no and have it be okay. Always get buy-in to share your views and recommendations because, otherwise, you're making it about you and your need to fix or save. Take a look in the mirror instead.

Examine what you've learned.

When we walk away from someone who is having a hard time, it's not always easy to switch back into a comfortable mindset. Take a few minutes to acknowledge what the interaction brought up for you. Did you find humility or discover how lucky you are to have your health, friends, clients, or family? Let those people know how much you appreciate them.

Take inventory of what you're feeling. Notice if the other person's situation brought up what you've been unwilling to see in yourself. What threatening or secret issues revealed themselves? Where can you go to find resolution? What have you discovered are the next steps in *your* evolution?

For instance, your coworker complains about being interrupted in meetings, something you've also experienced countless times. Is this a sign to speak up, leave the job, or get training to regain your power in those situations? A challenge has presented itself. Careful examination is being asked of you.

In the next chapter, you will be validated for your irritation with others. Feeling annoyed with someone doesn't mean you're a terrible person, it means there's information you need about your connection with them. Instead of "letting them know how you feel" or "letting them off the hook," see how my turnaround technique works for you.

This will shift your momentum where it needs to go for greater focus and productivity.

CHAPTER 2

HOW TO DEAL WITH PEOPLE YOU CAN'T STAND

Another barrier to inner peace is the challenge of dealing with people you cannot stand. It's okay to admit it. Most of us have someone who has influence on the ugly direction of our thoughts. Even their online presence can cause an allergic-like reaction. You might ruminate over them when you're stuck in traffic, in the shower, or lying restless in bed. These people don't live with us, but all too often, they follow us home in our minds.

Your focus on these irritants might seem irrational. You might want to chastise yourself for not being nice, but don't beat yourself up further. The methods you've been taught to "get over it" often do not work when dealing with grating individuals. At best, they're a temporary fix. Bottling up what bothers you is pointless.

Anger, confusion, and hostility will live in your bones and haunt your psyche until you're willing to acknowledge they exist. When that happens, you must choose your actions and words wisely. You don't want to regress to age 13. You want to call on your adult self and have control over the fixations of your mind.

To begin, let's examine how the general public reacts when people get on their nerves. It's fitting to start with the advice given to everyone who has ever had this problem:

Just let it go.

This cliché expression is used to shrug off discomfort, yet it can be a dangerous way to dismiss what bothers you. When irritation persists, take it as a sign—there are benefits waiting to be discovered. If you flick away this frustration, it's sure to return in other forms. You can erase people from your life and social media, but that doesn't mean they'll cease to exist in your thoughts.

When Disney's *Frozen* theme song, "Let It Go," became popular, I became fixated on the title and rejected it. Not only was I peeved at the message urging kids to "conceal, don't feel, don't let them know," I worried that it would perpetuate silent dysfunction in families across the nation.[1] It took a video of my friend's daughter belting out this beloved tune to make my hackles go down. I started to appreciate the liberation this song set forth. I know it's about self-empowerment, but still, telling a disturbing thought to simply "go away" doesn't work for many.

Some people can "let it go" with ease, but when you're apt to probe at a problem, keep going until you learn why it bothers you.

Redirect your thoughts.

This practice requires you to catch when your thoughts are strained. You have to stop when it hurts and decide to take a new direction. This is why affirmations and mantras have been useful for centuries. People chant and pray—to purify their thoughts and align with what they want.

My therapist, Joyce Follingstad, has a distraction phrase that works wonders for her, "I don't have to go down that alley right now." Reminding yourself that you have a choice could be all that it takes to boost your sense of empowerment.

If the choice to redirect your thoughts sounds logical, you could give it a try, but if you're anything like me, you'd rather sit there and pick at the emotional scab.

Notice if you're projecting.

When you project onto other people, you take the qualities (both good and bad) that you're unable to admit exist within you and assign them onto others. For instance, you might think someone is arrogant and condescending, yet those qualities might be true of you as well.

You've likely heard the saying, "When you point a finger at someone else, there are three fingers pointed back at you." That's a cool illustration of projection; nevertheless, it's not always true. For example, my mother seethes with anger when people don't say "thank you" for a gift. At the same time, she is the queen of sending cards of appreciation. She never misses an occasion. And, there's my friend who freaks out when people stare at their phones while walking down the street. She wouldn't be caught dead doing that! She's cautious.

Questioning if your criticisms are actually projections can be a touchstone in your self-development and can ease your tension. But remember, this technique might not bring you to an honest resolution.

Find their human goodness.

Surely, you appreciate that everyone faces battles in their lives. If there's a person you cannot stand, you could probably still name their good qualities. You know they matter to someone. Seeing their beauty can help soften your judgment, but does it stop you from being provoked by them?

A client once mentioned a guy in her office whom she avoids like the plague. Once he starts talking, he doesn't realize that no one is listening. Even if there's no eye contact, he sticks around wanting to get chatty.

Turns out, he had a traumatic brain injury in his twenties which makes it hard for him to read body language. When my friend got the backstory on this guy, she felt like a shrew for having such disdain for him. She was able to empathize and understand him more, but it didn't stop her from needing to set firm boundaries and place limits on their conversations.

Damn. What else can you do?

Yep, this can be a dilemma. These models of surrender aren't 100% reliable, and because of that, you might walk around with low-grade irritation that affects your sleep, food choices, and productivity. When it comes to dealing with people I can't stand, here's how I've learned to manage:

There's a business coach who wears a superhero cape in her social media videos. I'm not even linked to her, but when one of my contacts likes or comments on her videos, she reappears in my newsfeed like a fly who cannot be swatted.

Until I finally blocked her, what I saw in her videos would sidetrack my productivity and distract me from thinking kindly for hours!

I tried to listen for the jewels of her message. She must be sharing something of significance; however, I couldn't hear anything except a melodramatic "me, me, me." Even when she credited others, it somehow became all about her. It's almost like a magic trick. Do you know people who can do that?

I tried to "let it go," but my chilly disgust for this woman refused to be thawed. I tried to steer my thoughts in a more uplifting direction. That didn't work either. I tried to list what I'm grateful for and give compassion to myself. That seemed forced and fruitless.

So then, I asked if maybe I was projecting. What about this woman deserved such harsh judgment? Was it possible that I had the same issues as she? Am I offensive in the same way?

If I was projecting, I would have been unwilling to admit that the Cape Lady and I might actually be alike, yet we are indeed similar. I like to celebrate my victories, gather online support, and tell my stories; however, I make a faithful effort to notice how often I'm centering myself.

Finally, I tried to find the good and see her as human. That wasn't hard, but it felt superficial. She might be the next Mother Teresa for all I know, yet even that saint has been criticized.

The blocking feature has been a lifesaver for me, not always because I need protection from other people, but rather, they deserve to be safeguarded from my unspoken scorn. Plus, if my words became public, I wouldn't be proud of what I had to say.

I'm guessing there's a part of you, too, that doesn't rest well in discomfort, and thankfully so. Our progress gets blocked when we're consumed by frustrating people. We want to change them or teach them a lesson, but ultimately, we have no control over their thoughts, words, and actions—only our own.

Great. What now?

For heaven's sake, don't seek "positive" people in an attempt to feel better. It almost goes without saying, but I mention it because they'll detour your advancement. You must choose a safe person to practice this technique of dealing with people you can't stand. Here's how this goes:

Hit your breaking point.

Recognize when a person has invaded your thoughts. If you can't stop thinking about what someone has said or done, don't blame yourself for not getting over it. Don't question if your judgments are fair or correct. It's time to get pumped because you're about to flip the switch on this situation—big time!

Call a trusted skeptic.

For the sake of faster progression, pick up the phone for a quick chat. Find a skeptic, realist, critical thinker, or longtime friend. Make sure it's both private and confidential. If you email each other, this process can take too long and lose its momentum. Also, email leaves a risky paper trail. Same with texting—words can get lost in translation and come back to haunt you.

When critical thinkers join forces, it can be cathartic because there's no censorship needed. You won't have to say, "I don't mean to be rude, but . . . ." Just let it rip!

Do you see what I see?

To demonstrate the next step, here's a conversation with Üma Kleppinger, a truth telling author, writer, friend, and former yoga teacher. Üma left the yoga community because she felt as though skepticism and raw honesty were not permitted. That was a deal breaker for her. When I'm craving a no-holds-barred assessment, Üma always delivers a poignant insight.

> ERIN: I need your help. There's a coach on social media. I'm trying to understand why she bothers me. Can you take a look at her videos? Here's the link.
> (Ask them to describe what they see without your opinion or influence.)

ÜMA: I don't like that she claims to be a superhero. You know who is a superhero? The guy who grabbed the gun from the Waffle House shooter in Nashville. The single parent who works three jobs to put their kids through school, pay rent, and buy food. Those people are superheroes.

ERIN: Yes! I feel the same way!

ÜMA: The whole superhero theme reeks of privilege and make-believe. Helping people in business doesn't make you a superhero. Bringing clean water to Flint, Michigan? Now, that would be a real superpower.

ERIN: Yes! Thank you.

Knowing I wasn't alone in my reaction to the Cape Lady was validating. It told me I had insight into what others may have been feeling but couldn't say out loud. Üma's response narrowed down my frustration. The next question became—how do I get Cape Lady out of my head?

You might feel relief after venting and think you're all good. I'm begging you, do not stop here! You're about to be rewarded even more.

Write down what you heard.

My chat with Üma helped me to name what my judgments were about the Cape Lady:

a. savior complex
b. constant self-centering
c. arrogant privilege

I wrote this on a Post-It note and kept it hanging in my office. It served as a projection warning, and it kept me asking, "What real-life superheroes could use my support? Where can I sit back and listen today? How can I use my privilege to invest in others?"

Advocate for what you believe.

Minutes later, Üma sent a link to a story about Ayesha Rosena Anna McGowan. She's on a mission to become the first ever African-American pro female road racer. To us, she was a true superhero. When Ayesha landed on the scene, the Cape Lady vacated my thoughts. Üma and I marveled at Ayesha's gumption. She made us want to go smash a glass ceiling somewhere!

I could have posted a snarky message on LinkedIn about coaches who wear capes, lambasting, "Who do they think they are?" Thank God I didn't because it would have been a seventh grade stunt. Instead, my spirits were lifted by the sight of Ayesha triumphantly dominating in an industry skewed toward men. Üma and I continue to send each other links of authentic superhero stories. It's been gratifying to honor those we believe are cape-worthy.

Do you see what just happened there?

If I would have pretended the Cape Lady didn't bug me, and if I had refused to face my judgment, it would have continued to fester indefinitely. It would have caused me to be more disgusted with humankind. This may be why some people become bitter in their older years, or at any age. With no outlet to express what bothers them, their anger never finds a healthy release.

Give yourself freedom to find meaning in the things that piss you off. Then, you can find purpose in your fury, even when they aren't founded in kindness or truth. The result is you cease to dwell, and instead, move forward with your own convictions. Handle this privately and strategically.

Keep your core values updated.

When considering people you can't stand, realize it's because they represent the *opposite* of your core values. Through them, you can find your ultimate code of conduct. By letting these conflicting situations arise, you can see what burning topics mean the most to you now. View people's abrasive behavior as a sign to pay attention to what you hold dear.

- You're appalled at people who never put away their phones.
  CONNECTION is a core value.

- You're offended by people who always act happy.
  TRANSPARENCY is a core value.

- You get annoyed with groupthink and jargon.
  ORIGINALITY is a core value.

- You can't stand being around cheap and stingy people.
  GENEROSITY is a core value.

* You're tired of mean and arrogant drivers on the streets.
  TOLERANCE is a core value.

* You're puzzled why your neighbor doesn't wave or say hello.
  KINDNESS is a core value.

* You've had it with those who want everything done yesterday.
  PATIENCE is a core value.

* You get angry when rules are harsh and unbending.
  CONSIDERATION is a core value.

* You're sick of inflexible supervisors who micromanage.
  FREEDOM is a core value.

Another person's perceived downfalls can show you where you need to take action now. Consider this axiom: "Judging a person does not define who they are. It defines who you are." Judging a person can also inform what steps you should take in your own life.

- You feel outraged at people who text and drive.
  SAFETY is a core value.

  Besides putting away your phone when you're behind the wheel, find places in your community where safety is needed. Give to a homeless or domestic abuse shelter. Volunteer to be the doorkeeper at a local event.

- You're fed up with friends who refuse to leave their unhappy marriages.
  INTEGRITY is a core value.

  Take a hard look at your own life to see where you're faking it out of fear. What do you tolerate because you feel stuck? Who are your role models for sincerity? Keep your eyes on them and emulate.

- You feel angry when you see cliques and people being excluded.
  INCLUSIVITY is a core value.

  Find a class on diversity, equity, and inclusion. Learn how to speak up about the need to include and respect all types of people. Find out how you exclude and oppress, whether it's intentional or not.

* You get annoyed when people don't keep their commitments.
  DEPENDABILITY is a core value.

When someone completes a task or shows up for you, let them know how grateful you are. Applaud your friends who have finished a book, race, or any milestone. In the meantime, check your email to see who is still awaiting your reply.

* You get peeved when people gossip and demean others.
  RESPECT is a core value.

Take a coworker out to lunch, ask others to share their opinions, offer to help an elder, demonstrate what it means to listen and respect yourself enough to have boundaries and protect them.

* You are disturbed by those who burn bridges and cannot be faithful.
  LOYALTY is a core value.

Loyalty means you're there for good times and bad. If a coworker's dog dies, call to see how she's doing. If your family member is having a birthday, be the one who never forgets. List three people who have been the most loyal to you and let them know how much it means.

* You are disgusted by one-hit wonders and rookies who make it big.
  MASTERY is a core value.

  Don't hire people to do things cheaply. Pay extra for a professional with experience. Give yourself patience to learn skills that can be practiced forever—like golf, drawing, or learning an instrument.

* You can't stand people who are fake on social media.
  AUTHENTICITY is a core value.

  Support people and companies that use real people in their ads instead of stereotypical beauties. Recognize those who dare to be honest. Question when, where, and around whom you're pressured to conform or pretend.

* You've had it with bullies, abusers, and those who protect them.

COURAGE is a core value.

Do you want to be able to spot an abuser and know how to stop them? What does it mean to speak truth to power? Find teachers who can teach how this is done and demonstrate how to bring back your authority.

When you feel irritated, don't act on it immediately and don't brush it off, either. Use this turnaround technique and watch how it shifts momentum back to your work, relationships, and purpose. It's normal to not like people, but you can't let them derail what you came here to do.

The next task requires you to turn inward and take inventory of the unanswered questions in your head and the pain you might feel. It's time to find some resolution.

CHAPTER 3

HOW TO FIND SPACE TO REFLECT AND REBOUND

How do you know when to step back and gain perspective? When do you feel the need to be left alone? What signals tell you to back away from an interaction?

For many of us, it's when we can no longer pretend to be happy. We can't fake being nice, even if we try. We can't get over what happened. We're desperate for a good cry. We're stuck in a loop of worry and speculation, and it's hard to see the best in anything. We feel angry, impatient, and tired.

Instead of throwing unresolved anger in inappropriate places, would you like to learn how to contain it, understand it, and then use it constructively? You start by finding space for yourself, whether that's emotional, physical, or mental space.

Desiring this separation doesn't mean you want to hide. It doesn't mean you don't value your relationships or don't want to give back. It doesn't mean you lack emotional intelligence or resiliency. It means you need to rediscover your center and activate your highest thinking away from the noise that surrounds you.

We all need space to process the events in our lives. This reprieve could be essential for you on a weekly, monthly, or quarterly basis. You might start with the belief that something is wrong with you or that another person is intolerable. Accept that and know you're about to gain access to the bigger picture.

In this chapter, we'll take a look at why it's so hard to carve out time for personal recovery. You'll see how the demands of society keep telling us to "keep going" and "don't give up" despite internal alarms begging us to stop. You'll also learn the role solitude plays in creativity and productivity.

It takes guts to look at ourselves up close. Cynics and fundamentalists don't want to discover the truth, but a healthy person will seek honesty even when it's a blow to the ego. This is how we become accountable for our next round of changes—we look at what's difficult, and we agree to spend time there.

In a conversation with Ingrid Kincaid, she told me a story that's used in her course called Hidden & Forbidden Wisdom. It's about a man who lost the only key to his house. For hours, he searched under a street lamp on his hands and knees. A friend came by to help, and after a long time of unsuccessful searching, the friend asked, "Are you sure you lost it here?" The man replied, "No, I lost it over there." He pointed to the darkness. The friend questioned, "Why are you looking here?" The man said, "Because this is where the light is."

What a brilliant way to demonstrate how strongly people hang onto their beliefs that "love and light" are the ultimate answers, even when it keeps them from achieving their goals. Wearing rose colored glasses, they ignore what's bothersome to create a reality that's impervious to pain. This keeps them disconnected and in denial.

Dr. Sunshine Kamaloni writes, "Whoever tells you, 'keep going, don't give up,' should first be willing to look at your hurt and handle it in their hands. Only then can they earn the honour of saying such things to you. Because if they can't appreciate where you have been, how can they appreciate what it means for you to keep going?"[1]

In the documentary *Mister Rogers & Me*, Amy Hollingsworth tells a memorable story about this cherished television icon. She says young Fred Rogers was afraid to go to school because he was bullied for being shy and overweight. While he was walking home, kids would shout, "We're going to get you, Fat Freddy!"

Mr. Rogers explained, "What happened next was even worse. The grown-ups that were supposed to take care of me would say 'Act like it doesn't bother you. Act like you don't care.'" He continues that even as an eight-year-old, "I knew that wasn't right. I wanted permission to be angry."[2]

This example demonstrates why many people walk around with unhealed wounds and are unable to handle conflict. We are advised to forget and move on. We're guided to take the high road, rise above negativity, and not take things personally. In business, we're told to serve others and to set our needs aside. This simplistic thinking infuriates me because it's a missed opportunity for growth on just about every level.

Anguish is information, and discomfort is an invitation to develop new skills. The hurts we experience don't always evaporate over time, but with age, we can become mature enough to work with them. That's what we're aiming to do right now!

Another reason it's hard to find space is because we demand too much from these moments of respite. We think a weekend getaway will be enough to save our marriage. We expect a seven-day cleanse to make us skinny again. We live in a quick-fix society that wants overnight success. Health, relationships, careers, and self-development take *consistent* effort, and our hurts deserve thoughtful time to heal. Our questions merit patience in order to hear the real answers.

My drawing teacher, Phil Sylvester, talks about how the act of drawing has enabled him to study both his inner and outer world—documenting what he's seeing *and* feeling. He teaches art students how to slow down, follow their curiosity, and inspect the complexity that's in front of them. I learned from Phil that it's never our marks or materials that are inadequate, it's the struggle to observe and the need for instant results. That's what shackles an artist's enjoyment.

Plus, isn't emotional strife the source of notable art? In the Netflix movie *Kodachrome*, a photographer depicted by Ed Harris speaks of the misery in the lives of Hemingway, Picasso, and Jimi Hendrix. He declares, "No art worth a damn was ever created out of happiness, I can tell you that much."[3] These artists slowed down enough to study the complexity of their worlds, and we benefit from the creative expressions that came from it.

Perhaps we expect transformation to be quick because we're unpracticed in facing the tough stuff. That's why we cling to leaders who exemplify humility. Each time they tell us where they've screwed up, they give us permission to do the same. We all need help with something. All of us are limited in some capacity.

Do you realize 1 in 6 Americans has mental illness?[4] It's both maddening and cruel that we don't speak openly about this. Mental health should be required education in schools as well as management and workplace training. We are missing out on understanding the reality of what it's like for others. I suspect that's why suicide rates continue to rise. Positive inspiration cannot save them, but our wisdom about their struggles might.

A meme that I saw online said something like "Bipolar: It's a brain disorder that causes mood swings, which means it's not about thinking positive enough or 'snapping out of it' or about avoiding negativity." After reading that, I wondered if positivity pushers would be willing to change their message knowing there are people who are incapable of just flicking on the happy switch, whether they're medicated or not.

Dr. Daniel Amen, brain specialist and psychiatrist, released some alarming statistics:

* Mental illness ranks as the top stigmatized illness in the U.S.
* 1 in 2 are frightened by people with mental illness.
* 4 in 5 think it is harder to admit to having a mental illness than other illnesses.
* "Psycho," "nuts," and "crazy" are the most common descriptions of those with mental illness.[5]

It's no wonder those with anxiety, mood, or eating disorders suffer in silence. It's the same with those who are on the spectrum or have depression, bipolar,

PTSD, attention deficit, borderline personality, or obsessive-compulsive disorders. Functionality can be tenuous, and yet, there are standards we expect of everyone. Even those with full capability often fall short of this functional bar that we believe is attainable for all, if only they tried hard enough.

With tens of millions of Americans getting diagnosed each year with mental illness, when will we choose to become informed? What's it going to take for us to collectively take interest and to reset expectations for ourselves and humanity? Our refusal to embrace these unspeakable factors of life cause harm each and every day.

"One in three American women experiences domestic violence or stalking in some point in her life." The most common response people have when hearing this is "Why doesn't she just leave?"

In Leslie Morgan Steiner's TED Talk, she rationalizes why: "It's incredibly dangerous to leave an abuser because the final step in the domestic abuse pattern is 'kill her.' Over 70% of domestic violence murders happen after a victim has ended the relationship, after she's gotten out, because then the abuser has nothing to lose." Leslie explains that when we ask, "Why doesn't she just leave?' that's code for "It's her own fault."[6]

This is reason #876 why I despise oppressive positivity. If you were being harmed, would you want to be told to stay upbeat, be grateful, learn to forgive, and focus on your blessings? That can be a cruel response to a serious situation. Plus, it's easier for people to claim a woman is lying or exaggerating, than to admit the men they know may be abusive.

My editor, Christy Weber, survived breast cancer in her forties. In support, people told her to "keep fighting" and "stay positive." Their encouragement came from good intentions, but as Christy told me, "Cancer patients are led to believe they will kill themselves if they don't stay positive. This creates a debilitating form of guilt where we have to hide our true feelings because it's too painful for those who are watching."

As if having cancer isn't hard enough, patients are required to censor themselves to shield others from the discomfort of their disease. If someone tried to silence you in that manner, wouldn't you be angry? Empathy and strength are needed in these situations.

In an article titled, "Why We Need to Talk about Death and Dying," author Judith Johnson says, "Other societies educate their members about the reality of death and the processes of dying and grieving. We do not. We are left to figure it out for ourselves, relying on doctors and funeral directors to tell us what to do when we're face-to-face with death." She lists two jaw-dropping statistics:

1. 80% of Americans do not put their personal affairs in order before they die.
2. Only about 5% of Americans preplan their end of life rituals.[7]

It's no wonder we struggle for space to reflect. It can bring up issues that are scary to face. That's why most people stay busy and ignorant. They sweep addictions, illness, and dysfunction under the rug, only to accumulate more filth. Take comfort in the fact that, eventually, it catches up with them. None of us can skirt around these issues for long. The truth finds a way to present itself.

The New York Times writes, "In 1997, Tarana Burke sat across from a 13-year-old girl who had been sexually abused. The young girl was explaining her experience, and it left Ms. Burke speechless. That moment is where the Me Too campaign was born."[8]

As the woman to thank for #MeToo, Tarana Burke, an African-American civil rights activist, told abusers that they will be discovered and made it possible for victims to gain strength, find community, and reclaim their power.

Shame expert John Bradshaw says, "Healthy shame knows it needs community, love, and friendship."[9] That's why 12-step programs are successful, and the same with therapy or support groups.

When our limitations and traumatic experiences have no company, they get passed down through generations because no one feels equipped to handle them. When Aunt Judy dies from drinking and driving, or Cousin Larry gets busted for child pornography, no one discusses alcoholism, male privilege, or pedophilia. They focus on the person's positive attributes because, otherwise, they might feel accountable. Since history is never dealt with, the family dysfunctions live on.

If kids are going to learn how to admit when they're wrong and ask when they need help, adults will have to demonstrate how it's done. I've heard it said, "Happiness is not the absence of problems, it's the ability to deal with them." Go to therapy with pride and tell your kids, "Getting professional help is healthy. It makes me better at everything I do."

Alex Pang discussed his upcoming book, *Rest: Why You Get More Done When You Work Less*, on Jocelyn K. Glei's podcast, *Hurry Slowly*. Alex spoke about writer's block and how he doesn't believe in it. He said when he struggles for words, "It's because I haven't spent enough time in the gathering state. I haven't developed the data set that I need."

That's when Alex takes deliberate time off. "It's not about lack of skill or that I can't complete sentences. It's because I'm missing some information."[10] This is the freedom he needs to create. This outlook mirrors my writing experience, too. Breaks are essential when writing a book. Until I can synthesize the information for each chapter, my fingertips will refuse to follow.

Corporations tend to believe that the more time you spend laboring, the greater the result. They also think creativity comes from brainstorming with others and wrestling with ideas until solutions make themselves known. I'm a believer in Alex Pang's advocacy for solitude in order to let the subconscious process. That's how I prefer to move things forward. You, too?

Arianna Huffington is another activist for rest. Her *New York Times* bestseller, *The Sleep Revolution: Transform Your Life One Night at a Time*, is about "how our cultural dismissal of sleep as time wasted compromises our health and our decision-making and undermines our work lives, our personal lives—and even our sex lives."[11]

Sleep, rest, meditation, time alone, and even daydreaming help us make better decisions and feel at home with ourselves. That's why you must have awareness of what's going on with your body and emotions. When it's time to pull the plug, here's what you need to remember:

Guard your bad mood.

Meryl Streep famously said, "Guard your good mood." Guard your bad ones too, for everyone's sake. Unplug from social media. Don't answer the phone. Delay sending emails. Set notifications to auto-reply. Go on a long walk. Lock yourself in a room.

This might be impossible on some days, but in order to become emotionally well, you cannot be oblivious to your frustration. Your goal here is to recognize when you're off, not deny how you feel, and find some breathing room ASAP.

If you have to participate in life, practice staying as quiet as possible. Pretend you're on a silent retreat. Don't try to make small talk. Cloak yourself with an imaginary veil, so that your energy is permeable, but still contained.

Let people know, "You'll get a better version of me tomorrow. Do you mind if we postpone our conversation?" You can also try saying:

* I need time alone.
* I'm in a funk today.
* I'm in a quiet mood.
* I have a lot on my mind.
* I'm taking a mental health day.

If you have to lie, tell them you're sick. I cringe saying that. Why do we have to be sick to be left alone? I get it, though. As a kid, I was a pro at faking illness from school. One time in fifth grade, I chewed up Rice Krispies and chocolate, and spit them into the toilet because I desperately needed a day alone. My mom walked by, and I yelled dramatically, "Mom, I just puked!" Knowing she'd come into the bathroom, I had my evidence ready to go. Do what you gotta do!

Get your safeguards in place.

When you're in a healthy emotional space, talk to people who are closest to you. Let them know you'd like to set up "a system" for when you're in pain, crisis, or just a bad mood. Your requests could include:

    a. Don't ask me to solve any problems.
    b. Limit the amount of questions you ask.
    c. Don't hold me to any obligations or expectations.

You might want to put these into writing. When a loved one is going through hell, and you want to understand what's going on so you can help them, being able to view "the system" in print will remind them (and you) of how to act.

Let your safeguards know, they can request this process for themselves. All it takes are three words: Enact the system!

Say NO with confidence.

One of my pet peeves is when people don't RSVP or when they say "maybe" when they know they're not going to make it. Either way, it's a no-win situation. Your silence shows lack of graciousness, and your "maybe" says you don't have the guts to say "no." Why not give a real answer?

When you need to be alone, saying "no" is the kind thing to do. You might be afraid of hurting a person's feelings, but your soft "maybe" isn't going to help them either. It keeps you burdened with a task you don't want to do, and it leaves the host unable to plan. Part of self-care is saying "NO" when it's tough.

Before you decline, thank them for including you. That part frequently gets omitted, and it makes all the difference.

- "Thank you for thinking of me.
  I'm not able to make it. Hope we can
  reconnect soon."

No further explanation needed. (I'm still trying to learn that part.) When you give a lengthy justification, it doesn't actually help. A succinct "no" is enough.

Now that you've been able to secure your own space, the next chapter provides 12 ways to maximize your quiet time. These tools aren't designed to resolve all your issues, although that might happen with a few of them. It's more about letting the dust settle, getting clear with yourself, and calling forth the person you want to be.

When your efforts to feel better don't work, don't fall into the trap of believing that you're flawed or that you aren't trying hard enough. What matters is that you stop and find a way to get yourself back into gear. In the next chapter, we'll discuss what to do when you've found alone time. For some, these moments don't come around often. Would you like to maximize them?

CHAPTER 4

HOW TO MAXIMIZE YOUR TIME SPENT ALONE

Now that you're ready to give yourself space, here are 12 exercises to get you back into your power. In these precious moments of solitude, others might suggest you get some exercise, find your creative muse, or get your house organized. These are all valid ideas; however, you've likely heard them a million times.

The 12 strategies you're about to learn aim to be unique. They came from favorite books, my teachers, and my own ways of maximizing alone time.

1. Savor your solitude.

When I got divorced at age 30, my brother Shawn gave me advice that was groundbreaking at the time, "Savor this time of being alone because it won't happen again for many years." Back then, it was assumed I'd get remarried and eventually have children. Thirteen years later, neither has occurred, partially because I embraced every minute of my aloneness and didn't ever want it to end. It's one reason I'm a self-employed ghostwriter. This life-style of needing isolation is luxurious to me, most of the time.

Novelist and playwright Paul Rudnik offers a comical description: "As a writer, I need an enormous amount of time alone. Writing is 90 percent procrastination: reading magazines, eating cereal out of the box, watching infomercials. It's a matter of doing everything you can to avoid writing, until it is four in the morning and you reach the point where you have to write. Having anybody watching that or attempting to share it with me would be grisly."

How does alone time look for you? If you wouldn't be interrupted or seen by anyone, what would happen in your alone time? Don't just dream it in your head. Get specific about what you need to feel restored. What would you like to eat, drink, watch, listen to, or do? Write it down and find a way to make it a reality for yourself.

2. If I really tell the truth.

We all feel tired and overwhelmed at times, yet decisions still need to be made every day, and we want them to be sound.

Author and educator Ingrid Kincaid teaches an exercise designed to strip away confusion and evoke a sense of honesty to your most pressing issues. Ingrid is known for her directness and clarity, which is why people flock to her to face the choices they need to make next.

She explained to me how she advises students to get a legal-sized, yellow-lined notepad and on the first line write, "If I really tell the truth . . ." and see what words follow. Then, on each new line, start again with the opening phrase. Do it multiple times until you can't go any further.

FOR EXAMPLE: You're upset that your boss takes days to return your emails. It's reached a point where you're irritated and think she's ignoring you. You want her to know this is bothering you, but should you really say something? And if so, what, when, and how?

> If I really tell the truth . . . my boss doesn't respect me.
>
> If I really tell the truth . . . it seems like I don't matter.
>
> If I really tell the truth . . . this has been happening for months.
>
> If I really tell the truth . . . it's causing me to question my worth.
>
> If I really tell the truth . . . I'm losing interest in this job.
>
> If I really tell the truth . . . I don't even like this industry.
>
> If I really tell the truth . . . I want to have a fulfilling career.
>
> If I really tell the truth . . . my boss isn't the problem.
>
> If I really tell the truth . . . I'm afraid to make a job change.
>
> If I really tell the truth . . . I need help finding what's next.
>
> If I really tell the truth . . . it's been years since I updated my resume.

> If I really tell the truth . . . I want to be
> gone by November.

There you go! No need to confront the boss. Contact a career counselor or recruiter instead. This exercise works wonders, especially when you don't skip writing out the lead phrase and you do it in longhand. By repeatedly summoning the truth from yourself—brain to heart, heart to hand, hand to pen, pen to paper—honesty has a chance to slowly break through the confusion.

3. Get to know your anger.

I was in my car turning left onto a narrow Portland street when an angry cyclist appeared at my windshield. He seemed to be infuriated with me. Being somewhat comfortable with conflict, my first response was to roll down the window and prepare for a rumble with words.

He pointed and screamed, "Next time, stay in your own lane!" I yelled back, "Next time, don't be such an angry biker!"

I wanted to insult him and make him question himself because that is what I believed he was doing to me. My response lacked bite and decorum, but that's what flew out of my mouth. He rolled his eyes and pedaled away.

Truthfully, I *did* cut that turn short. That gentleman's anger was reasonable. He was fearful of losing his life. My hunk of steel versus his 15-pound bike? Come on! I parked the car and recognized there was anger brewing inside of me, and it wasn't about the cyclist. There was a laundry list of grievances swirling in my head that had reached critical mass.

Now, this is where most people stop. They might sense their guilt and replay the scene in their head, but they usually brush it off by saying, "That's just how I am" or "It was just a bad moment." I've tried to rationalize my anger by claiming it's the Irish in my blood. That doesn't excuse me from having to evaluate it.

The Anger Control Workbook, by Matthew McKay, Ph.D., and Peter Rogers, Ph.D., regards anger as a two-step process.

Step 1: Pain occurs – This can be either physical or emotional—a stubbed toe, spilled coffee, car accident, excessive traffic, stomachache, late fee, disagreement at work, or a burnt dinner. Pain can arise from loss, frustration, rejection, or a threat to your safety.

Step 2: Thoughts follow – "These are interpretations, assumptions, and evaluations of a situation that make you feel victimized and deliberately harmed by others. Trigger thoughts blame and condemn others for the painful experiences you've suffered."

Pain + trigger thoughts = anger

"It's like a can of gasoline, and your trigger thoughts are the match. . . . Pain by itself doesn't ignite rage, and trigger thoughts without pain are like a match without fuel."[1]

PAINFUL MOMENT: A cyclist gets mad at me + TRIGGER THOUGHTS: What was his problem?/ What an ass!/All bikers are mean./It wasn't my fault./How dare he yell at me!/These streets are too narrow./I did nothing wrong! = ANGER

Again, this is a stopping point for most people. It's as far as they're willing to go because if they look any further, self-accountability would be needed. They'd rather maintain a superior opinion of themselves, which turns them into raging critics and passive-aggressive victims.

I parked the car, and fresh thinking began:

- Wait, I might have overreacted.
- I shouldn't have yelled back.
- What a lame reply.
- Hope no one saw.
- Hope he's okay.
- Where was my impulse control?
- Why did I have to be critical?
- I did cut that turn short.
- Probably was speeding, too.
- That was unsafe.
- I wasn't being present.
- That was dangerous of me.

If you can see the part you played in an argument, way to go. Others choose to feed their resentments and have their untrue beliefs confirmed. They'll come home and make blanket statements like, "Damn bikers, they all have a chip on their shoulder!" This is a shortsighted way to exist. Feelings of anger can lead you to make changes in key areas of your life.

Your anger might be also be completely justified. As a woman, I've been told that it's unladylike to lose my cool. I've been punished for showing my true emotions. Not just women, but many people from marginalized groups have been on the receiving end of disgraceful injustices and discrimination. In those cases, the only accountability you need is getting help for yourself. Don't let anger become who you are. Don't let anyone steal your joy for too long.

Try this technique when you're angry.

Start with the question: "At the time of feeling angry, what was my fear?" Then, form the next question and the one after that based on your answer.

a. Identify the fear your anger provoked.
b. Name what you can do to tame that fear.
c. Ask where that fear or theme appears in other parts of your life.
d. Consider what's in your control to change.

Unresolved anger doesn't hide. When it shows up, it can remind you how you can do better, what you are missing, and when you should seek proper support. You might be surprised at what your anger will reveal. Some say it's a cry for the things we love most.

4. Take steps to heal heartbreak.

My general practitioner, Dr. Kayla Luhrs, says in her email newsletter, "On the emotional spectrum, heartbreak is one of those deep movers and shakers: nothing else I've encountered so powerfully grips my core and pushes me to the brink of true reflection."[2]

I imagine all of us have experienced heartbreak in some capacity, whether it's the loss of a partner, child, friend, job, home, sibling, or dream. Bottom line? It can throw you off center for days, weeks, months, or years. Even if you are the initiator of a breakup, the heartbreak can be unbearable. Perhaps it's the price we pay for the love we have received. This quote from *The Little Prince* speaks truth:

> "Of course I'll hurt you.
> Of course you'll hurt me.
> Of course we will hurt each other.
> But this is the very condition of existence.

To become spring, means accepting the risk of winter.
To become presence, means accepting the risk of absence."

Having managed a self-help bookstore, I am happy to report there's one book that excels in soothing grief and heartbreak, *How to Survive the Loss of a Love*. The authors knew what they were doing when they created this gem. It's a small book that doesn't need to be read cover to cover. They knew the attention span of their readers would be short, so everything is laid out in bullet points, tiny chapters, and bite-sized paragraphs. The best part? Poetry is sprinkled in-between—ranging from soulful to snarky.

"Thursday:
drowning in love

Friday:
drowning in doubt

Saturday:
drowning

Sunday:
God, I can't drag my

self to church this morning.
Please make a house call.

*

"I remember thinking once
that it would be good
if you left because
then I could get some
important things
done.

Since you've left I've done
nothing, nothing
is as important
as you."

*

"At a critical moment I said:
'I would rather you go
and regret your going
than stay
and regret your staying.'
Someday I'm going to
learn to keep my mouth
shut."

*

"I'd have a nervous breakdown,
only
I've been through
this too many
times to be
nervous."[3]

Relationship author John Gray created an exercise, "The Feeling Letter," to help us sort through the explosion of feelings that occur after heartbreak. I've used this numerous times to honor the totality of what occurred with a person. It can also be developed as an actual letter that you send to a loved one.

The Feeling Letter

1. For Anger
I don't like it . . .
I feel frustrated . . .
I am angry that . . .
I feel annoyed . . .
I want . . .

2. For Sadness

I feel disappointed . . .
I am sad that . . .
I feel hurt . . .
I wanted . . .
I want . . .

3. For Fear

I worry . . .
I am afraid . . .
I feel scared . . .
I do not want . . .
I need . . .
I want . . .

4. For Regret

I feel embarrassed . . .
I am sorry . . .
I feel ashamed . . .
I didn't want . . .
I want . . .

5. For Love

I love . . .
I want . . .

I understand . . .
I forgive . . .
I appreciate . . .
I thank you for . . .
I know . . .[4]

After a product for my business failed to convert into sales, I wrote a "Feeling Letter" to myself. Devastated at first, I was able to move on with clarity about what went wrong *and* right. Organizing and giving voice to my feelings also served as a spark for what needed to happen next.

When you try this exercise, choose your words carefully and let yourself edit them. When your emotions run high, you can't always communicate effectively. This exercise allows you to review, refine, and make sure each statement reflects the truest essence of how you feel.

Notice the final prompt for each section begins with "I want . . ." or "I know . . . ." If you gathered those responses and took them to a therapist or coach, it would give you a head start in naming and claiming your goals. They will enable a counselor to get to know you more quickly. There are multiple benefits to this self-help process.

5. Let your regrets be known.

I once did an online survey asking, "Which of these topics interests you most: suspicion, regret, anger, betrayal, confusion, guilt, resentment, or loneliness?" Regret was the undeniable winner!

Research professor Brené Brown said, "Like all emotions, regret can be used constructively or destructively, but wholesale dismissal of regret is wrongheaded and dangerous. 'No regrets' doesn't mean living with courage, it means living without reflection."[5]

It can be humbling to face your errors, make amends where necessary, and commit to gradually improving. My regrets are often from when I was unable to see a person for who they really are. I hate learning lessons the hard way, especially when the truth was staring me in the face the whole time.

In an article from *Inc.*, "How to Get Over Regrets, According to Science," author Jessica Stillman mentions an experiment from the National Institutes for Health. She writes, "To figure out how best to handle life's shoulda-coulda-wouldas, the research team asked study volunteers to try one of three interventions:"

1. One group "did nothing special."

2. Another group "was prompted to write what a compassionate and understanding friend might say about their regret."

3. A final group was asked to "write about their own strengths and positive qualities."[6]

Can you guess which group achieved the most relief? Those who wrote compassionately said they experienced "more self-forgiveness, personal improvement and self-acceptance. It turned out that accepting your flaws is better than trying to boost yourself up by focusing on positive qualities," reports PsyBlog.[7]

We all have room to improve. Every one of us. Have you seen *An Autobiography in Five Short Chapters* by Portia Nelson? Her poem gives us grace to see our downfalls and make steady progress to avoid them.

I.

I walk down the street.
There's a deep hole in the sidewalk.
I fall in.
I am lost . . . I am helpless.
It isn't my fault.
It takes forever to find a way out.

II.

I walk down the street.
There's a deep hole in the sidewalk.
I pretend I don't see it.
I fall in again.
I can't believe I am in the same place.
But, it isn't my fault.
It still takes a long time to get out.

III.

I walk down the street.
There's a deep hole in the sidewalk.
I see it is there.
I still fall in. It's a habit.
My eyes are open.
I know where I am.
It is my fault. I get out immediately.

IV.

I walk down the street.
There's a deep hole in the sidewalk.
I walk around it.

V.

I walk down another street.[8]

6. Realize the potency of PMS.

Gentlemen, this information is for you as well as the ladies. We need to talk about the days leading up to a woman's period—often referred to as Premenstrual Syndrome (PMS). It's been said this is when a woman becomes unstable, unpredictable, unkind, and unable to properly rationalize.

As a woman, I've heard these comments for years about myself and other women. Now, I realize they are riddled with misogyny, lies, and a hint of truth. Allow me to explain:

Remember the exchange between Donald Trump and Megyn Kelly during the first GOP debate and the blood comments that followed? Megyn asked candidate Trump about his comments on Twitter calling women "fat pigs, dogs, and disgusting animals." She inquired, "Does that sound to you like the temperament of a man we should elect as president?"[9]

With that question, she brought stern honesty to the table. She challenged a male candidate to take ownership of his words and to consider if they had presidential quality.

The next day, Trump said Megyn had "blood coming out of her eyes, blood coming out of her wherever."[10] He tweeted that she "behaved very badly," "was the biggest loser of the evening," and "was not very good or professional." He also called her a "bimbo."[11]

For women nationwide, this was an all too familiar scenario. We've been in Megyn's shoes before. If we ask a ballsy question, demand accountability, bring up a sore subject, we tend to get shamed much like Mr. Trump did to Megyn.

I'm not saying Megyn was hormonal or bleeding, but to me, her inquiry was most definitely a PMS kind of question.

The week before a woman starts menstruation is her most intuitive and transparent time of the month. PMS week can be hard for women (and those around her) because our filters have been removed. The curtains of truth have been ripped opened. Whatever has been lingering emotionally makes itself known, whether we want to see it or not. Sometimes, it's manageable. Other times, it's not.

Historically, men have tried to control women by blaming their bold opinions and brash ideas on their periods. And you know, they were partially correct. A woman's hormonal cocktail during this time informs her of what critically needs to change in her life. It's easy to see why it's been viewed as a threat to the opposite sex.

When a woman is about to start her period, she remembers what she buried inside and didn't want to face. We view PMS as a syndrome, a temporary form of insanity. In reality, it can be a woman's most honest and courageous time of the month.

Questions for premenstrual women—in the week before your period, do you become:

Intolerant of your partner's drinking?
Maybe it's time to say something.

Disgusted with your kids' attitudes?
Maybe you should seek family counseling.

Tired of your friends who gossip?
Maybe you need to weed the friend garden.

A woman in her PMS power has the ability to end dysfunctional relationships, stop abusive situations, and summon the bravery to walk away from those who don't respect her, if she chooses to do so.

If you notice each month that a woman in your life gets feisty, this is her true self. She means what she says, even if her delivery is sharp and she denies it a week later. Her hormones will always be ebbing and flowing, so get used to these fluctuations until she hits menopause. That's when she will officially lose her filters and become even wiser.

Ladies, when you're gearing up to bleed, take time to be alone! Try not to be a loose cannon, but also *take yourself seriously.* Do not discard what you feel; however, use caution in sharing with others.

I saw a report stating that four out of ten parents never talk to their daughters about menstruation.[12] To learn about women's cycles, check out Suzanne Mathis McQueen's book, *4 Seasons in 4 Weeks: Awakening the Power, Wisdom & Beauty in Every Woman's Nature.* At the end of each chapter, there's a section for men on how to support a woman during each week of the month.[13] This book is essential for young women to own. It helped me learn self-care and gain body confidence.

7. Use laughter for relief.

Do you ever find yourself taking things too seriously? Does your mind often race with pressing questions and opposing views that feel crucial to address? Yeah, I can relate. That's why we need to laugh as much as possible. In your quiet time, find a way to listen to, read, or watch something to add levity to your situation.

Years ago, I heard that local, spiritual author John Conley was dying of cancer. Remembering how jovial he was when we met, I wondered if he'd talk to me about his upcoming death. We wound up recording the interview and posting it publicly. I can't find the recording anymore, but I did keep a printed copy of the email he sent to his subscribers.

John wrote, "Now, of course, I know absolutely nothing about death and dying. But I am dying, which gives me at least some credibility. Or at least, I am supposed to die. Yes, I'm supposed to die in the next year or so. But, then again, I was supposed to die last September. Death can be so unreliable. Anyway, you can listen to my interview with Erin Donley right here: *Really Wise Interview with John*."[14] Thank goodness for those who can bring humor to death!

A Forbes article says there are health benefits to laughter similar to antidepressants. Laughter releases endorphins, causes a burst of brain activity, and can even help with inflammation.[15] Could that be why John Conley is still alive today, almost eight years later?

8. Look out different windows.

As I write this today, Anthony Bourdain has just passed away. To encapsulate his legacy, his words have been circling the internet:

"If I'm an advocate for anything, it's to move—as far as you can, as much as you can, across the ocean, or simply across the river. Walk in someone else's shoes or at least eat their food. It's a plus for everybody."

When I'm in a funk, I try to stay overnight somewhere other than my home. With the Oregon coast, Columbia River Gorge, and Mt. Hood all nearby, my outdoor scene can change drastically within an hour. To make the most of my getaways, I go for walks and try to spend time just staring out the window.

When I sold my house of 15 years, I could only see the past and the "old me" through those familiar glass panes. Landing in my new pad was like the first day of college—full of possibility. My senses came alive. I started playing my trumpet again and sketching musicians who played in bars in my neighborhood.

You don't always have to move or go far. One night away might be all it takes. Book a room at a cheap motel or splurge somewhere that's fabulous.

You might prefer to have time alone at home near what's familiar and convenient. Instead of you leaving, see if your children and partner can stay at a hotel or an Airbnb for a night. If you're a single parent, see if your child can sleep over at a friend's house.

What matters is that you take time for yourself and notice if your familiar scene is helping or hurting your personal growth.

9. Get inside your body.

The trumpet was my instrument of choice in fourth grade music class. I wanted to hang out with the boys and beat them in securing 1st chair. Today, I've just started taking lessons again from Joe Klause, a professional trumpet player.

Joe is teaching me how to re-learn this instrument as an adult. I've been studying how to improve sound quality, find the barriers blocking my breath, and discover emotions that may be hiding inside my body, but are now ready to be expressed.

If you've ever blown into a musical instrument, you know it takes effort, much like doing exercise or yoga. This has a noticeable effect on how you feel.

For example, when a family member was diagnosed with cancer, everyone was upset and concerned except me. I had complete trust that everything was going to be fine. Before his surgery, I wanted to send him a video of me playing the *Rocky* theme song on my trumpet. We both loved this movie as kids. The idea made me giddy.

As I sat down with the sheet music and began to play, I could barely get through the first line. My eyes welled with tears and a long sob followed. Turns out, I was worried too. My mind couldn't access grief because it had been hiding in my lungs. Breath pushed it out and made it known, and what followed was a profound sense of relief in my body—it lifted weight from my shoulders and revealed a deeper truth about how I was feeling.

In Chinese Medicine, each organ relates to a certain emotion.

Liver = Anger, frustration
Heart = Depression, restlessness

Lungs = Grief, detachment
Kidneys = Fear, insecurity

That's why heart-opening poses in yoga can make you feel relaxed, twists and side bends can release your frustration, and anything that gets your breath moving, such as sex, jogging, or biking, can feel euphoric. Getting into your body can be done with movement or meditation. In your quiet time, try to give your body what it needs to recognize and release emotion.

10. Loneliness can be lethal.

After a relationship ends, people will advise you to take a break before dating again. Every time someone mentions this to me, I have to explain how lonely I felt in my previous relationship. Why would I want to isolate more? Neil Young pinpoints this feeling in his tune, "Lotta Love":

> *So if you are out there waitin'*
> *I hope you show up soon*
> *'Cause my head needs relating*
> *Not solitude.*[16]

When you feel lonesome, it can seem like you're the only lonely person in the world. Everywhere you look, you see happy couples who seem madly in love and friends who frolic together in sync. Surprisingly, your loneliness has lots of company. Cigna surveyed 20,000 Americans:

47% feel left out.

46% sometimes or always feel alone.

43% feel isolated from others.

43% feel their relationships are not meaningful.

Whoa. Can you believe that? Instead of just encouraging people to be nice and generous, wouldn't it be smart to also include the facts on loneliness? Knowing that almost half the U.S. population does not have tight-knit connections makes me want to phone a friend or have lunch with a stranger.

Cigna says young people and the elderly are the loneliest. They also state that loneliness has the same effect on mortality as smoking 15 cigarettes a day, which makes it more dangerous than obesity. They linked loneliness to teen suicides, the opioid epidemic, and the safety of seniors.[17]

You can have friends, family, community, and a partner and still be lonely. Social media doesn't help with loneliness, either. It's a Band-Aid, at best. It's easy to collapse into loneliness because that can seem less stressful, but don't stay there long. Connecting with your people is what will ultimately restore your soul.

As morbid as it might seem, list 10 people outside of your family whose deaths would absolutely devastate you. Write down their names and keep the list visible to create a tangible reminder of your most precious relationships. Make a point to connect with these people—call them, send cards, make soup, run an errand for them, get coffee, or just inquire how they've been doing. Nurture these relationships, and when you're feeling lonely, you'll have your core people available to contact.

11. Learn to recognize dysfunctions, disorders, and disabilities.

There was a person in my life who would invite me to get close with sweet compliments and enticing texts. We'd enjoy moments of back and forth flirting, but inevitably, he would misinterpret my words, then lash out with insults and accusations. It shocked me every time.

He was a generous person with financial success and obvious charm, yet this pattern of verbal abuse kept happening between us. I began to question my words and second guess my sense of decency. I also became fixated on understanding his unpredictable behavior.

That's when I learned about narcissism, which at its root is an avoidance of feeling vulnerable. While the narcissist's public image might seem confident and capable, there's a constant state of hypervigilance in the narcissist's mind. They have a profound lack of trust in others.

We think of narcissists as having an air of superiority, an inflated ego. We might even refer to the ancient Greek myth of Narcissus who got stuck gazing at his own reflection. That image only helps to a point, but it doesn't reveal the hidden motivations at play.

It's impossible to feel good about ourselves all the time, though the narcissist will desperately try. They aim to gain power over others, so they can feel more powerful. Remember, vulnerability isn't an option for them. This pattern likely began in childhood as a way to cope with their circumstances.

As adults, narcissists are often resistant to therapy because it would mean making themselves vulnerable. In fact, narcissists are nightmare clients for therapists because they refuse to give up their power in order to get help.

A must-read book on narcissism is *The Wizard of Oz and Other Narcissists.* Author Eleanor D. Payson is a licensed marital and family therapist specializing in treatment for codependents who find themselves in various relationships with narcissists. This book helped me identify the one-way relationships in my life and challenge my need to stay in them.

After learning about narcissism, I stopped interacting with that narcissistic man. I stopped trying to be better for him. I quit asking friends what was wrong with him. Instead, I found a therapist to help me learn why I kept going back for more. Why did I think I could change him? What needed to change in me?

Do you think we should have compassion for narcissists? Perhaps, because to survive in their world, they need to have a façade. Losing control is unthinkable to them. That's a rough way to live, and it's also tough on those who love them because intimacy gets blocked. For a narcissist, every day is like the Beatles song "Eleanor Rigby": "Wearing a face that she keeps in a jar by the door. Who is it for?"[18]

There's another book self-help readers recommend called *Will I Ever Be Good Enough: Healing the Daughters of Narcissistic Mothers*, by Karyl McBride, Ph.D. When I worked at the bookstore, women raved about how this work confirmed their childhood trauma and helped them break the legacy of abuse in their families.

Years ago, we didn't seem to have labels for people's behavior. Now, there's more information about personality disorders, autism, mental illness, codependence, addictions, PTSD, and phobias. This can help us to make educated guesses about what a person might be facing, so we can gauge how to respond.

12. Fall back in love with yourself.

"Document the moments you feel most in love with yourself—what you're wearing, who you're around, what you're doing. Recreate and repeat," advocates Warsan Shire.

There's only one goal needed for alone time: Come back into yourself. We enter the world alone and will leave the same way. Finding self-love can be a lifelong challenge and a worthy pursuit. And at the end of the day, it's *your* reflection you'll see in the mirror.

Take inventory in your alone time of every area of your life—health, wealth, family, friends, and faith. Remind yourself of the few things that are within your control:

- How honest you are.
- How much you show appreciation.
- How kind you are to others.
- How you express your feelings.
- How good you are to yourself.
- How you interpret situations.

Nora Ephron offers some parting advice, "Above all, be the heroine of your life, not the victim." Find creative ways to pick yourself up and face your fears with ever-improving strategies.

In the next chapter, we'll talk about how to speak up when it's hard and how to be a voice for good. If you have the audacity to ask tough ques-tions and poke at the status quo, your words aren't always going to be welcomed. They often have consequences. This calls for a chat about timing, delivery, and discernment.

CHAPTER 5

HOW TO USE YOUR VOICE TO DO GOOD

Politics and religion have always been taboo topics. At holidays, it's not uncommon for a family leader to declare there will be NO politics at the dinner table. That's been the rule of thumb in business, too. Today, that request is hard to achieve. Political disagreements in America are less about policy and more about the harmful words we are saying to each other—online and offline.

If you found out your words (or lack thereof) were unintentionally causing harm, would you want to know what you're missing? I keep wondering, perhaps naively, can these heated times somehow influence us to become kinder people? What would it take to make that happen?

I've seen enormous healing take place when truthful conversations happen. Scary talks that we don't want to have are sometimes the most satisfying experiences. When you can hear and express what's been hidden inside for way too long, the feeling is often indescribable.

In 2012, I was granted access to a TV studio at Portland Community Media to film my very own talk show. *Reveal What's Real* ran on Portland cable channels and still exists today on YouTube.

The show addressed topics that were sensitive and complex yet begged to be discussed. I wanted each show to be an invitation to those who were curious. Titles included:

"What Doctors Don't Say About Stage Four Cancer"

"The Penis: What Lovers Need to Know"

"Is Motherhood Really for You?"

"Does Monogamy Seem Unnatural?"

"Self-Sabotage: Don't Shoot Yourself in the Foot"

These were my own contemplations at the time, and they were issues I was hearing at the bookstore, online, in women's groups, and with friends. When recording these shows, I often felt emotional about the topics—not like I wanted to cry, but rather, my passion would come across as frustration, impatience, or sarcasm.

No matter how hard I tried to be socially pleasing, someone would take offense. For me, the criticism was worth it because the pain of silence was far worse. In order to expose these topics, caution became key.

Choose Your Words Wisely

Have you ever sent an email or posted a message online that was misunderstood, taken out of context, or shouldn't have been said at all? Have you lost sleep, a relationship, or an opportunity because your words got you in trouble?

You might have felt guilty after it happened. You might have questioned if you could have handled it differently. But it's likely you were told not to take it personally or that you weren't responsible for how others responded. Normally, I'd want to examine how these statements lack accountability, but there is *some* truth to them. People will see you through their own lens, and you'll see them through yours.

A study from the *Journal of Personality and Social Psychology* says we have only a 50-50 chance of assessing the intended tone of a writer. How we interpret their tone comes largely from our moods and stereotypes, which are often ignored and full of unconscious bias. The same study reveals that 90% of the time, we think we've correctly interpreted the tone of the writer.[1] This leaves a dangerous gap in communication.

Do you ever want to shut another person down with your perspectives?

Do you want to unleash rage online about what you've experienced?

Do you refuse to be silent about issues that matter to you?

These are normal responses to today's political climate. But what if, this time, you approached it in another way?

Can you choose not to lose it?

Can you set better boundaries?

Can you be angry without shaming or blaming?

Can you walk away without attacking or feeling attacked?

For years, I've praised and recommended the book *The Verbally Abusive Relationship*, by Patricia Evans. Finding her material was like discovering the Holy Grail. She provided answers to questions no one had been able to answer for me. In 1992, Patricia made her debut on *The Oprah Winfrey Show*. Since then, she's been contacted by over 47,000 verbal abuse targets, mostly women.

Patricia described to me how verbal abuse isn't just name-calling. It negatively defines a person. It tells them who they are and what they think, feel, and want. That's why it lacks credibility and arouses counterattacks. It's a specific form of language.

After Trump was elected, I booked a consultation with Patricia to examine how and why verbal abuse occurs. Once and for all, I needed to know when verbal abuse was happening to me, when I was the one doing it, and why people choose to speak like this in the first place.

Verbal abuse is a lie told to you or about you. You might have been told you don't care, you're stupid, no one likes you, you'll never change, you make no sense, you don't know what you're talking about, you're too sensitive, you're not yourself, or that you are worthless.

Once again, do you see how these statements aim to tell you who you are, what you think, how you feel, and what will happen in the future? That's how you can distinguish verbal abuse from truth telling or an angry outburst. It's also how you can distinguish if someone's feedback (or your own) is crossing the line.

It feels good to let off steam. We all have the right to state our opinions, even when we're angry and want to disagree. It turns into verbal abuse when a person habitually lies, tries to distort the facts, or categorizes people into unfair stereotypes. Verbal abuse is a lame way to communicate because it doesn't even represent the truth. It's make-believe, and yet, it still causes real harm.

Know Who You're Dealing with

An important part of understanding verbal abuse is grasping the reality in which the abuser lives. This makes their motives clear. To summarize what I've learned from *The Verbally Abusive Relationship* and my conversations with Patricia:

Reality I = Dominance & Control

Abusers live in Reality I, where they seek dominance and control. If they lose the upper hand, their anger mounts. Second place isn't an option. Not even for a moment. They believe "It's my way or the highway."

Reality II = Mutuality & Co-creation

People in Reality II seek compromise, empathy, respect, and honesty. These people make space for each other's needs while having healthy boundaries. Reality II strives to retain individuality and gain understanding as it forms togetherness.

Can you see how badly these worlds collide?

It helps to know—it's impossible to argue with an abuser. They don't have the ability to visit Reality II because retaining their dominance is of prime concern. In fact, when abusers get called out, they're often shocked. If they reflect on their actions and admit to harm, that means a loss of dominance. They must have control.[2]

Verbal Abuse Online

Whether you're a Trump fan or not, I have to let you know, his words are often perfect examples of verbal abuse.

June 19, 2018, Trump tweeted about his zero tolerance policy on immigration. This is just one example of his consistent verbal abuse: "Democrats are the problem. They don't care about crime and want illegal immigrants, no matter how bad they may be, to pour into and infest our Country, like MS-13. They can't win on their terrible policies, so they view them as potential voters!"

Let's break that down, shall we?

* "Democrats are the problem." (blaming)
* "They don't care about crime" (telling Democrats how they feel)
* "and want illegal immigrants," (telling Democrats what they want)
* "no matter how bad they may be, to pour into and infest our Country, like MS-13." ("infest" implies these human beings are vermin)
* "They can't win on their terrible policies," (predicting the future)

- "so they view them as potential voters!" (telling Democrats how they think)[3]

Only you can know what you feel, think, and want. And no one knows the future. This is why some Americans are compelled to battle against this verbally abusive leader.

What's most tragic about verbal abuse is our natural response. Targets of abuse feel exhausted. They often give up and start mimicking the communication of the abuser. Because it worked for the abuser, they believe it's effective for them too. That's why you see some who oppose the President fighting back in the same abhorrent way.

Verbal abuse conjures a mob-like mentality. It gets people to bond against a target as the primary goal. We need to bring verbal abuse into our awareness to preempt groupthink and prevent escalation.

How to Call Out Verbal Abuse

In phone sessions with clients, and also in her writing, Patricia teaches how to respond constructively to verbal abuse. She's told me each situation will be different, but when you hear something that resembles verbal abuse, stop the person and ask:

* What did you just say?
* Did you just tell me what I am?
* Can you repeat that?
* Did you just tell me what I do?
* How do you know my future?
* Wait, say that again, so I can put it on video.

By asking a person to repeat, you can step back and see verbal abuse for what it is. Then, Patricia would advise you to say, "Guess what? You're not me, and you're not God, so you don't know what I am/think/feel/want." If you've been targeted, this is a simple reply you can choose. After this effort, no more words need to be said because that would be addressing absurdity.

Again, don't forget—abusers don't want to understand or form togetherness. You will lose when you start explaining yourself. You might think, "If they knew how I felt, they'd take back what they said." No, it doesn't work that way. That's why silence is often a solid response to verbal abuse. Save your breath.

When Silence Reigns Supreme

Here's a good example of choosing silence to gain strength: I was asked to make a speech about the marketing and sales industry at an entrepreneurial camp for teens. Delighted, I prepared the specs that were given: 15 minutes to describe my career trajectory and the remaining 45 minutes for questions from the teenagers. Knowing that I was affecting the next generation, I took extra measures to craft a speech that would resonate.

When I arrived, a gentleman, let's call him Bob, came over and said he would be presenting along with me. He explained he had been a counselor at this camp for over 20 years. I was relieved to have a veteran joining me on stage.

Before we began, Bob asked if I could take the lead. He said he'd introduce himself, then turn it over to me since he'd done this "a million times already." Bob started with a brief statement about his career, maybe two minutes long. As he was talking, I noticed how the teens weren't listening. I couldn't even understand what the hell this guy did for a living. Something about floor tiles and trade shows.

When it was time for my shtick, I saw the teens' eyes light up, along with their brains. The synergy became apparent, and I was having fun, too.

About four minutes later, Bob interrupted me while in mid-sentence. "I'm going to have to stop you there. Let's turn the program over to the kids and hear what they have to say." At first, I thought he was joking. Remember, I was told to speak for 15 minutes before questions began. The kids looked confused and unprepared. I wasn't even halfway done, but for some reason, Bob had heard enough.

I was livid and confused, yet I didn't want that to come across in my body language. Because of his old-timer status at the camp, I acquiesced and wondered if I had said something wrong or if I misunderstood the instructions.

After the program, I texted a friend who was there. He recognized what happened and later called to say that Bob was a notorious bully. My friend asked if I could meet with the group leaders to share my example of this man's mistreatment. Turns out, several members of the organization had a bone to pick with this guy, but they were too timid to speak up. And Bob wasn't the only bully. My friend hoped I could open important dialogue about this unspoken issue. At this point, I considered my options:

a. I could confront Bob the bully myself.
b. I could tell the organization what happened.
c. I could drop the whole thing and move on with my life.

None of these choices seemed useful. Confronting a bully who lives in Reality I is a fruitless venture. When abusers get called out, they usually make a joke of their behavior and laugh at your response. They see the issue as your weakness, not theirs.

I could tell the organization about my experience, but I had given enough to these people. Speech preparation took time, attending the event took time, and the phone calls that followed took even more time. Plus, this experience impacted my sleep and social enjoyment. Did I want to invest *more* in this situation? Not really. Great, so you might be guessing I just let it go. No way!

Do you know that classic tune by Aaron Neville, 'Tell It Like It Is?' I've always loved that line:

> 'If you want something to play with
> Go out and find yourself a toy.
> Baby my time is too expensive
> And I'm not a little boy.'[4]

As a grown woman, my time is precious, so is my health, business, and relationships. I don't need to rescue this organization from bullies, nor do I feel called to teach this man a lesson. I wanted to publicly humiliate Bob and get revenge, which might not have been a *wrong* choice, but in the end, I chose to save myself.

This experience revealed how much I enjoy working with teens. Where else can I donate my time to them? I was also reminded this isn't the first time someone has tried to pull a power play on me. I want to serve as a positive example to others who are put in these situations. Wouldn't it be incredible if one day, I could teach teens how to respond to abuse, privilege, and oppression? I still have some learning to do, but that's a long-term project that excites me!

Let's Talk About Public Humiliation

I often think about public humiliation and question the value it serves. Once, on LinkedIn, I noticed a man replying inappropriately to a post about a woman's career accomplishments. His statement wasn't about her work, it was about her beauty. He called her "ravishing and delicious." My instant reaction was to publicly chastise him.

I can't remember what I said exactly, and the post has since been deleted, but when my anger subsided, I wondered if I could have handled it differently. Was I too harsh? Should I have let that woman defend herself?

To gain perspective, I asked my LinkedIn community how they would have responded to this guy's offensive comment. I wondered if there were best practices or a standard code of conduct for calling out people on their outdated behavior. The comments were fantastic.

Marvin Fjordbeck, an attorney and consultant, offered a professional way to reply: "While it's tempting to challenge someone I don't know, my better self would ask questions that start with, I wonder. 'I wonder why you chose not to comment on the person's ideas. And why did you choose to comment on appearance?'" Marvin said that when you shame someone without knowing more, it can take you down an uncertain path. By acting curious, you can get your point across and push them to have to answer for themselves.

Eli Bonilla, a marketing and social media specialist, provided this insight: "First, do my words honor my own truths and respect those who have been done harm? Second, are my statements written in a way that holds the capacity to be heard? If both are a yes, press post."

Keri Caffreys, a human resources analyst, said, "You don't have to degrade yourself and stoop to their level, but you can certainly tell them what they said was offensive. And . . . ignorance does not excuse inappropriate behavior."

Malcolm Boswell, a business and employment economist, offered another generous reply: ". . . you reacted with rightful indignation, and maybe took it a bit far, but YOU recognized it, and that shows character. Bravo! #MeToo gets validated by women like you that stand up in a measured, yet strong way."[5]

Managing Conflict and Confrontation

Bill Eddy is a lawyer, therapist, and mediator who created a method for responding to high-conflict people. His book, *BIFF: Quick Responses to High-Conflict People, Their Personal Attacks, Hostile Emails, and Social Media Meltdowns*, is a quick read that will change the way you approach conflict forever.

Mr. Eddy has seen his share of arguments—in domestic settings, neighborhoods, online, and in the workplace. That's how he came to know and designate "High-Conflict People (HCPs)." His books explain their patterns of behavior, the personality disorders they exhibit, and how a person can effectively respond to them. Developed by Mr. Eddy, the BIFF Response® Method stands for:

Brief
Informative
Friendly
Firm[6]

This systematic method for responding to HCPs has been extraordinarily useful to me. I once had to BIFF Response® a man on Twitter who came after me in real life. I found out he had contacted my boss and was calling our company's vendors to "warn them" that I could not be trusted. What the hell? This was a full-on attack from an internet troll.

Using the BIFF Response®, I sent an email in the friendliest tone possible, saying, "I heard you have concerns about me. If you'd like to speak directly, perhaps we could talk sometime. I'm willing to hear what's on your mind. Take care, Erin."

It's been over two years and he hasn't uttered a peep or a tweet. Did I want to freak out on him? Totally! Did I want to publicly humiliate him? OMG, yes! In this case, I chose the BIFF Response® Method. It shut him up without having to attack or threaten back.

Once I helped a fellow ghostwriter use the BIFF Response®. She told me about her client's family who was upset that she was writing a tell-all memoir. They decided to target my friend the ghostwriter with threatening letters in the mail and online insults warning her to back off from this project. Instead of trying to reason with these people, we put together a BIFF Response® letter of resignation.

"Thank you for letting me know about the concerns associated with the upcoming memoir. After considering your feedback, I've decided the conditions of this opportunity aren't going to work for me. Here is the material we've created, of which Pam owns exclusive rights. Take good care."

Thankfully, she never heard from them again. We still high-five today about the professionalism and lack of emotion we were able to conjure at that moment, especially since this family made some troubling accusations. Many HCPs have disorders, such as narcissism or borderline personality. Being able to spot HCPs and respond with skill can save you financially, mentally, and even physically.

Coach and speaker Rachel Beohm teaches communication tools that help make daunting situations easier to handle. When it comes to ranting online or wanting to scold another person, Rachel explains that shaming others might change their brain and behavior, but it doesn't make them think.

When a person is shamed, blamed, or dominated, their brain goes into fight, flight, or freeze. They can't access their higher thinking, which can cause them to miss the point entirely.

For instance, when Rachel's young daughter ran into the street without looking, Rachel instinctively grabbed her and screamed, "No!" That might have shocked or scared her enough to never do it again, but it didn't teach her that streets and cars are dangerous. It just taught her that Mom panics if she runs into the street. Having a thoughtful conversation about what happened and why it was dangerous is essential for a lasting change of behavior.[7]

This is true for adults as well. We can't shame people into doing what is deemed right, fair, or safe. Shaming doesn't work and can be emotionally harmful—same with passive aggression, sarcasm, name-calling, or mean jokes. There has to be a line drawn in the sand.

With that said, if there's a person threatening you or deliberately trying to hurt you, it's your right to say whatever you want to them. No one is going to fault you for that, and I'd never tell anyone to treat their abuser with respect. But, if you feel guilty when you attack online, and you want to evolve how you communicate when you're upset, here are some exercises that have helped me.

Before You Send or Speak

Years ago, I created a discernment process with my mentor, Ingrid Kincaid. When I was having a difficult reaction to someone, I'd write an unedited response letter. Then, I'd go through the five questions. Answering these before hitting send helped me to monitor my intentions, edit my message, and prepare for the consequences of my words.

1. What selfish need does this fill?
2. How will this benefit others?
3. What do I secretly hope will happen?
4. What do I secretly fear will happen?
5. Am I willing to face the consequences?

When you're feeling stressed about a difficult email or interaction online, take a few minutes to write down whatever you want to say. Don't hold back! This will reveal your true thoughts and help you pinpoint exactly what might get you into a snafu.

Question 1: What selfish need does this fill?

Don't get tripped up by the word "selfish." It's not meant in a negative way. It's used to help you get boldly honest about your intentions. Do you want to be right? Do you want to teach this person a lesson? Do you want to get someone in trouble? Do you want to prove their lack of knowledge? Do you want to make them feel ignorant? Are you doing it for shock value?

If your selfish need is rooted in dominance and control, it's important to see that. You can still choose to deliver your message, but know that you're intentionally choosing words that further the division between people.

Conversely, if your selfish intention is to bond with another, feel better about a situation, gain clarity about what happened, or find out what a person meant, then acknowledge that, too. The key is not to pretend.

Question 2: How will this benefit others?

You'll never really know exactly how your message will be helpful or not, but still try to identify if there's a benefit for anyone besides you. If not, that might be okay, or it might be a red flag. Just notice.

Question 3: What do I secretly hope will happen?

Get clear about the expectation you would like to see. Do you want your message to create change, build trust, break through, or boost your image? Speak truthfully to yourself about your best-case scenario.

Question 4: What do I secretly fear will happen?

What's a realistic, worst-case scenario? If your message aims to pry into a delicate issue or challenge a problem because it must be addressed, there may be pushback. What are you afraid will happen?

Question 5: Am I willing to face the consequences?

Having taken yourself through the self-editing process, you can tell by now if your intention, expectations, and outcomes are survivable. If they are not, you can still move ahead with your original message, but get ready for the backlash that might follow.

I have to warn you—even if you're confident, honest, clear, and kind, that doesn't mean your message will be understood and appreciated. But if you're happy with how you come across and you've told the truth to yourself, then you might not care what follows. Whatever the response, it won't rattle you.

After answering the five questions, you might decide you're better off picking up the phone or meeting in person to reach an understanding. You could also wait a few hours or days to see if your answers are different or no longer necessary. Timing, medium, and method of delivery are all important to consider.

An Example of Discernment

A client gave me permission to share her story. Cherise is a freelance business consultant who was contacted by a former client of hers. This person needed advice ASAP about a pressing issue she was facing.

Cherise was slammed with project deadlines but felt obligated to help this person for the sake of the relationship. She was irritated by the way this woman asked for help. From the woman's voicemail, the request sounded to Cherise like a demand on her time that was expected at no charge—an implied favor.

She composed a lengthy reply, explaining how she's buried in work and filled with family obligations, and she'd have to put off *paying* clients, but she'd be willing to help anyway. Using the email she had crafted (but hadn't sent), we went through the five questions:

What selfish need does this fill?

Cherise admitted she wanted to be liked by this client. She also wanted her to know that she's busy and in demand, so her time should be appreciated. She didn't want clients to assume she could be available for unpaid advice.

How will this benefit others?

She thought it would help her client see how presumptuous it was to assume Cherise could drop everything and work for free.

What do I secretly hope will happen?

Cherise hoped the client would email her back with apologies and insist on paying extra for the work since it was required on short notice.

What do I secretly fear will happen?
Cherise feared she'd run out of energy and that this client wouldn't appreciate her extra efforts when all was said and done.

Am I willing to face the consequences?
Not really. That's why Cherise called me to formulate a new message—one that might accomplish her goals and soothe her fears. Remember, when you're having an emotional reaction to something, it can be a difficult to respond without passive or active aggression. We ditched Cherise's letter. Instead, she wrote:

"Thanks for contacting me. I'd be happy to provide the guidance you're needing. With requests that require immediate turnaround, I charge 15% more than my standard fee. If that works for you, I'll start rearranging my schedule. Please let me know before 5pm today."

TAKEAWAYS:

1. She was able to uncover her expectations and get them met.
2. She saw that her business policies needed to be revised.

3. She came up with a new plan for last minute clients.
4. She made it clear how to do business with her.
5. She regained her dignity and set a new boundary.
6. She was able to teach this client how she wanted to be treated.

Good news followed! Cherise's client replied to the email with massive thanks and told her to send an invoice right away. She said, all along, she expected to pay the extra fee and was thankful. Regardless if that was true or not, when Cherise made her expectations calmly clear, the client respected her needs.

We think we can hide our emotions and intentions, but much of the time, they come through anyway in our body language, tone of voice, and choice of words. By checking in with yourself, you can get clear about the risks that you face.

Is There Missing Information?

The things we do not say eventually get in the way. That quote makes me recall an obituary that gained national attention. After a woman named Kathleen passed away, her grown children sought revenge. The announcement said Kathleen had abandoned her kids and became pregnant by her husband's brother.

"She passed away on May 31, 2018 in Springfield and will now face judgment. She will not be missed by Gina and Jay, and they understand that this world is a better place without her."[8] Ouch!

The most common response online was to cheer for the survivors. I imagine these supporters might have been neglected as children or had a nightmare parent. Revenge stories are often empowering, yet this obituary was sad for me.

Could Kathleen have been suffering from mental illness? Could she have been raped or abused by one or both of these brothers? Leaving her children might have saved her life or theirs. We'll never know.

To me, that obituary said more about her adult children, rather than who Kathleen might have been as a person. If they had a chance to hear their mother's truth, perhaps apologies would have happened all around. Maybe they could have softened their hearts to the pain felt from a life spent apart yet bonded in blood?

Kathleen's obituary prompted another question to add to the self-editing process.

Question 6: Do I have all the information needed about this person or situation?

Much of the pain we feel is from the stories we've created to explain why the pain exists. Instead of asking a person, "Can you tell me what happening for you?" it's common to keep silent and assume your perception is correct.

Sorry, Not Sorry

It's never too late to make amends, or at least, forgive yourself.

Is there someone in your life who needs to hear from you? Are there any apologies you've been wanting to make? Anne Frank said, "Dead people receive more flowers than the living ones because regret is stronger than gratitude." Don't wait until it's too late. Whether your apologies are overdue or unexpected, start giving them out freely as an offering of kindness. A simple "I'm sorry" could suffice.

After an altercation, you might say, "I screwed up. What I did wasn't okay. I used poor judgment. I wasn't thinking. I apologize." Avoiding saying, "I'm sorry, but . . ." because your apology won't be heard any longer.

If you find yourself getting emotional about how you did this person wrong, stop right there. Your sense of accountability is admirable, yet try to apologize without making it about you. It's about the hurt you caused, not the hurt you felt.

Author and speaker Sam Horn tells people to take the "AAA Train": "Explaining why something wasn't done when it was supposed to be done makes people angrier because explanations come across as excuses. Instead, Agree, Apologize, Act."[9]

Watch how often you say you're sorry. Is it truly necessary? Women are notorious for over-apologizing, especially in the workplace. This can be viewed as a weakness. When you've been corrected, when you've miscalculated, or when you've messed something up, choose these alternatives before saying sorry:

* Great catch! I'll make changes immediately.
* Thanks for telling me.

* Gotcha! Glad to clean it up.
* Oops, must have missed that.
* Thanks for flagging my error.
* Happy to fix it now.

When apologies are needed, do you know how to restore trust? It helps to name what you did wrong, say how it affected the other person, and offer a way to make it good.

* *I can see that by being late, I put extra stress on you. That's unacceptable. Your feelings matter to me, and I'm truly sorry. It took guts for you to say you're upset with me. I will do better next time.*

* *When we were talking about your political concerns, I found myself wanting to prove you wrong. I'm profoundly sorry. I can see how my words shut you down and ended our evening on a terrible note. Hearing what's important to you matters. Will you give me another chance?*

Desiree Adaway teaches organizations how to restore community when their people have been hurt and offended. In an article, "Making Mistakes," she says, "To do the work required of social justice is to know that you're not perfect, can't be perfect, and that part of the process is learning how to fail and get back up—with grace and fortitude."[10]

End the Civil War of Words

I hope the information in this chapter makes you want to check yourself before you speak. With social media, it's easy to examine your tweets, comments, and posts from the past. Review what you've said. Notice the responses. What were your triggers? What topics set you off? Are you proud of how you handled yourself?

Stop before you speak and do some listening first—not only to yourself, but to others. It's healthy to be upset. Your outrage needs to be heard. Can you trust yourself, though, not to lose your cool and resort to verbal attacks?

Whatever privilege you might have—money, time, education, health, shelter, or mobility—know that you have the power to affect change and help others through personal accountability and your conscious choice in words. Slow down. Discover your biases. Stay awake. Become resilient. Stop doing harm. Let the civil war of words end with you.

In the conclusion of this book, we'll review the inner terrain you've covered to face your power and find your peace. There's one last step to go. You will be granted permission to "get out of Dodge" when it's time for you to leave a situation or relationship—no apologies or explanations necessary.

HOW TO KNOW WHEN IT'S TIME TO LEAVE

As we bring this book to a close, give yourself credit. You've signed up to uncover more about who you are, how you feel, and what you want. Perhaps now, negativity doesn't have to bother you. Positivity doesn't have to be your goal. You can be present for everything life has to offer. Let's review what you've learned so far:

- How to be present for another person's pain, and how it can make you kinder and wiser.

- How to deal with people you can't stand, and how your judgments provide clues about your values.
- How to find space to reflect and rebound, and how to fight societal pressure in order to return to yourself.
- How to maximize your time spent alone, and how it can reveal what drags you down and will lift you up.
- How to use your voice to do good, and how to stay responsive in the face of anger, abuse, and conflict.

Before you go, think back to Dee's story in the Introduction. Recall how her final days were spent releasing frustration from her past. By the time she found her voice, her time on Earth was limited; however, you still have a chance to get real about your desire for change.

Do you feel stuck in a job, city, friendship, home, or relationship?

Do you believe you need a valid reason to leave?

Do you agonize about how to explain your departure?

Do you worry about hurting people's feelings?

Do you want to make sure everyone's cool with you stepping away?

Knowing how and when to disengage has been an ongoing lesson for me. Oftentimes, I've needed someone to tell me it's okay to go. If Dee were here today, I believe she'd want you to know some basic rules. These are easier said than done, yet they are core requirements in achieving self-love, self-respect, and healthy boundaries:

* It's okay to say no.
* You always have the right to leave.
* You don't owe anyone an explanation.
* Let them be angry with you.
* You don't have to listen to abuse.
* Let them disagree with you.
* Your feelings matter, and you have a right to them.

When you face your longing for change, remember the tools you've been given in this book to find accountability, discernment, and understanding. When your inner strength is restored, you won't need others to tell you what to do. You'll know the answer in your heart. It might spark change, and it might also inform you of the need to stay, if even temporarily, to get your next moves in place.

At the end of the day, it's important to feel grateful for what you have. It's equally vital to assess what people, places, and choices no longer meet your needs. Make this part of your cleansing routine and do it with love. Integrity is a choice you can make at every turn—don't ever let anyone take that away from you.

ENDNOTES

Chapter 1

1. Ezra Klein, "Is Modern Society Making Us Depressed?" April 2018, in The Ezra Klein Show, produced by Vox, podcast, MP3 audio, 1:31:07, accessed August 23, 2018, https://player.fm/series/the-ezra-klein-show/is-modern-society-making-us-depressed.

Chapter 2

1. Idina Menzel, "Let It Go," track 5 on Frozen: Original Motion Picture Soundtrack, Wonderland Music Company, 2013, compact disc.

Chapter 3

1. Dr. Sunshine Kamaloni, email message to author, May 29, 2018.

2. Mister Rogers & Me, directed by Benjamin Wagner and Christofer Wagner (2010; New York, NY: PBS, 2012), DVD.

3. Kodachrome, directed by Mark Raso (2017; Los Gatos, CA: Netflix, 2018), https://www.netflix.com/title/80216834.

4. "Mental Illness," Health Information, NIH National Institute of Mental Health, accessed August 19, 2018, https://www.nimh.nih.gov/health/statistics/mental-illness.shtml.

5. Dr. Daniel Amen (@DocAmen), "End the stigma, mental illness is real," Twitter meme, March 27, 2018, https://twitter.com/DocAmen/status/978716004623831040.

6. Leslie Morgan Steiner, "Why Domestic Abuse Victims Don't Leave," filmed November 2012 at TEDxRainier, Seattle, WA, video, 15:53, https://www.ted.com/talks/leslie_morgan_steiner_why_domestic_violence_victims_don_t_leave.

7. Judith Johnson, "Why We Need to Talk About Death and Dying," HuffPost, November 17, 2011, https://www.huffingtonpost.com/judith-johnson/why-we-need-to-talk-about_b_682218.html.

8. Sandra E. Garcia, "The Woman Who Created #MeToo Long Before Hashtags," The New York Times, October 20, 2017, https://www.nytimes.com/2017/10/20/us/me-too-movement-tarana-burke.html.

9. John Bradshaw, "Healing the Shame That Binds You (Part 1)," YouTube video, 9:31, November 19, 2010, https://www.youtube.com/watch?v=5q2tZa1gp8Q.

10. Jocelyn K. Glei, "Alex Pang – Prioritizing Rest & Reflection," episode 12, January 29, 2018, in Hurry Slowly, produced by Hurry Slowly LLC, podcast, MP3 audio, 44:39, https://hurryslowly.co/012-alex-pang.

11. "The Sleep Revolution: Transform Your Life One Night at a Time," Arianna Huffington online, accessed August 19, 2018, http://arianna huffington.com/books/the-sleep-revolution-tr/the-sleep-revolution-hc.

Chapter 4

1. Matthew McKay, Ph.D., and Peter Rogers, Ph.D., The Anger Control Workbook, (Oakland, CA: New Harbinger Publications, 2000), 33.

2. Dr. Kayla Luhrs, "Moon News—Dancing in the Dark," email newsletter, April 15, 2018, https://www.moon cyclemedicine.org/so/9MBAPm3F?cid=eefc0231-c27d-437e-a51a-e713de7d862d#/main.

3. Harold H. Bloomfield, Melba Colgrove, and Peter McWilliams, How to Survive the Loss of a Love, (St. Louis, MO: Turtleback Books, 1993), 92–153.

4. John Gray, "The Feeling Letter: How To Communicate Difficult Feelings To A Loved One," Mars Venus, June 9, 2014, https://www.marsvenus

.com/blog/john-gray/the-feeling-letter-how-to-communicate-difficult-feelings-to-a-loved-one.

5. Brené Brown, "I've found regret to be one of the most powerful emotional reminders," Facebook, April 26, 2018, https://www.facebook.com/brenebrown/posts/2054129977935434.

6. Jessica Stillman, "How to Get Over Regrets, According to Science," Inc., July 15, 2016, https://www.inc.com/jessica-stillman/how-to-get-over-regrets-according-to-science.html.

7. Dr Jeremy Dean, "Move On Quickly From Regret Using This Writing Instruction," PsyBlog, July 5, 2106, https://www.spring.org.uk/2016/07/how-to-move-on-from-regrets.php.

8. Portia Nelson, "There's a Hole My Sidewalk," Autobiography in Five Short Chapters, (New York: Simon & Schuster, 2012), xi.

9. Kayla Epstein, "Trump responds to Megyn Kelly's questions on misogyny – with more misogyny," The Guardian, August 6, 2015, https://www.theguardian.com/us-news/2015/aug/06/donald-trump-misogyny-republican-debate-megyn-kelly.

10. Danika Fears and Beckie Strum, "Trump: Megyn Kelly had 'blood coming out of her wherever'," New York Post, August 8, 2015, https://nypost.com/2015/08/08/trump-megyn-kelly-had-blood-coming-out-of-her-wherever.

11. Rebecca Sinderbrand, "Donald Trump late-night angry-tweets Megyn Kelly, and it is epic," The Washington Post, August 7, 2015, https://www .washingtonpost.com/news/post-politics/wp/ 2015/08/07/donald-trump-late-night-angry-tweets-megyn-kelly-and-it-is-epic/?utm_term= .37b6d84aad3b.

12. "It's time we talk about periods – the importance of family dialogue to break the taboo," Essity, accessed May 18, 2018, https://www.essity.com/ company/essentials-initiative/stories/slices-of-life/ slice5-time-to-talk/its-time-we-talk-about-periods.

13. Suzanne Mathis McQueen, 4 Seasons in 4 Weeks: Awakening the Power, Wisdom, and Beauty in Every Woman's Nature, (Ashland, OR: Tobacco Road Press, 2012).

14. John Conley, email message to author, December 28, 2010.

15. David DiSalvo, "Six Science Based Reasons Why Laughter Is the Best Medicine," Forbes online, June 5, 2017, https://www.forbes.com/sites/david disalvo/2017/06/05/six-science-based-reasons-why-laughter-is-the-best-medicine/#7aa0405d7f04.

16. Neil Young, "Lotta Love," track 2 on Comes a Time, Reprise Records, 1978, Vinyl LP.

17. Jayne O'Donnell and Shari Rudavsky, "Young Americans are the loneliest, surprising study from

Cigna shows," USA Today, May 1, 2018, https://www.usatoday.com/story/news/politics/2018/05/01/loneliness-poor-health-reported-far-more-among-young-people-than-even-those-over-72/559961002.
18. Beatles, "Eleanor Rigby," track 2 on Revolver, Parlaphone, 1966, Vinyl LP.

Chapter 5

1. Christina Gillick, "7 Ways to Avoid Email Misinterpretation," American Writers & Artists Inc. online, June 7, 2012, https://www.awai.com/2012/06/7-ways-to-avoid-email-misinterpretation.
2. Patricia Evans, The Verbally Abusive Relationship, (Avon, MA: Adams Media, 2010).
3. Donald Trump (@realDonaldTrump), "Democrats are the problem. They don't care," Twitter, June 19, 2018, https://twitter.com/realDonaldTrump/status/1009071403918864385.
4. Aaron Neville, "Tell It Like It Is," track 1 on Tell It Like It Is, Parlaphone, 1966, Vinyl LP.
5. Erin Donley, "YOUR OPINIONS PLEASE: How do you feel about public humiliation?" LinkedIn, June 2018, accessed August 23, 2018, https://www.linkedin.com/feed/update/urn:li:activity:6410176737031913472.
6. Bill Eddy, BIFF: Quick Responses to High-Conflict People, Their Personal Attacks, Hostile Emails,

and Social Media Meltdowns, (Scottsdale, AZ: Unhooked Books, 2012), 15.

7. Rachel Beohm, interview by Erin Donley, June 2018.

8. David Mikkelson, "Minnesota Woman's Family Runs Caustic Obituary," Snopes, June 7, 2018, https://www.snopes.com/news/2018/06/05/minnesota-womans-family-runs-caustic-obituary.

9. Sam Horn, "Want to Know What to Say—When You Don't Know What to Say?" LinkedIn, April 25, 2018, https://www.linkedin.com/pulse/what-say-when-you-dont-know-sam-horn.

10. Desiree Adaway, "Making Mistakes," Desiree Adaway online, accessed August 19, 2018, http://desireeadaway.com/making-mistakes.

ABOUT THE AUTHOR

Erin Donley is a ghost-writer in Portland, Oregon who specializes in activism, self-help, and leadership books. She works with industry experts who want to challenge the status quo and rise above the noise with their words. She's written with professional athletes, high-profile speakers, corporate executives, spiritual teachers, and activists who want to share their powerful message with the masses.

For years, Erin managed a personal growth bookshop and wrote the store's profitable email newsletter. This allowed her to interview hundreds of thought-leading authors and to study the unmet needs and desires of self-help readers.

Erin was the host of the provocative Portland TV show, *Reveal What's Real*. She was also an award-winning sales executive in radio, a contributing writer at Huffington Post, and a sales advisor for keynote speakers. Today, Erin is emerging as a voice for verbal abuse education and diversity.

Besides writing books, Erin enjoys playing trumpet and power walking. She loves dogs, older people, warm vacations, and anyone who likes to have a good laugh.

To reach Erin for interviews or speaking, visit ErinDonley.com.

TALK TO ME!

What did you find helpful in this book? What ideas did it spark for you? What would you add to this topic? What would you like to examine next?

Please post your comments on Amazon and other book review websites. Your feedback means the world to me, and it helps others find this information.

Thank you,
ECD